Essential Motivation in the Classroom

When this book was first published, schools were under intense government pressure to improve, teacher morale was being constantly hammered by the Chief Inspector of Schools, the *Daily Mail* was proclaiming that exams were getting easier, standards were dropping and everyone was bemoaning the state of classroom behaviour. So, how much has really changed in a decade?

Enduring in its appeal to teachers at all ages and stages, *Essential Motivation in the Classroom* remains the definitive one-stop guide for teachers who want to know how to motivate children – and how children learn to motivate themselves. In the ten years since this book was first published, it has proven to be a best-selling text that informs, inspires and amuses educationalists around the world.

This updated and revised tenth anniversary edition continues to take the reader on a rollercoaster ride through the theories of teaching, learning and thinking. Ian Gilbert highlights his famous 'seven keys' of motivation, offering a range of strategies, ideas and insights to help learners become motivated from within.

An entertaining and inspiring read, this book is full of useful, practical advice, ranging from motivational research from leading theorists to philosophical gems from Homer Simpson. Teachers in all sectors of education will find this book indispensable, helping them to change the culture of their classrooms and improve the effectiveness of their teaching forever.

Award-winning **Ian Gilbert** is a leading educational innovator, speaker and writer. He is the founder of Independent Thinking Ltd, and the author of a range of best-selling titles including *Why Do I Need a Teacher When I've Got Google?* (Routledge, 2010).

Praise for the first edition

'I think the book is well suited to anyone who works with children and young people, either in formal educational settings or within the out of school environment. It gives a clear understanding of what is so often happening within the classroom, or within adult interactions with young people, and how this can be key in demotivating and blocking creativity and engagement of participants.'

Tricia Lee, Artistic Director, MakeBelieve Arts, London

'*Essential Motivation* is a wonderful, practical and inspirational book for any educator. Ian Gilbert is passionate about his subject and it is an enjoyable and informative read.'

Sue Oates, International Baccalaureate Primary Years Programme Coordinator, Aarhus Academy for Global Education, Denmark

'Ian Gilbert's book was helpful for me because it helped pull me away from traditional ideas about discipline. It helped me to think about what I am doing in class in a more nuanced and complex way – if I can get my students to believe in themselves, then they will want to learn.'

Anurag Jain, English teacher, London

'A very readable, concise book with many practical tips for creating that "X factor" that is essential to student achievement.'

Pete Reeves, Community Learning Manager, Dawlish Community College, Devon

Essential Motivation in the Classroom

Second edition

Ian Gilbert

Routledge
Taylor & Francis Group

LONDON AND NEW YORK

First published 2013
by Routledge
2 Park Square, Milton Park, Abingdon, Oxon OX14 4RN

Simultaneously published in the USA and Canada
by Routledge
711 Third Avenue, New York, NY 10017

*Routledge is an imprint of the Taylor & Francis Group, an
informa business*

British Library Cataloguing in Publication Data
A catalogue record for this book is available from the
British Library

Library of Congress Cataloging in Publication Data
Gilbert, Ian, 1965-Essential motivation in the classroom /
Ian Gilbert. -- 2nd ed.p. cm.Includes bibliographical
references and index.ISBN 978-0-415-64354-2 (hardback)
-- ISBN 978-0-415-64355-9 (pbk.) -- ISBN 978-0-203-
07900-3 (ebook) 1. Motivation in education. I. Title
LB1065.G48   2013370.15'4--
dc232012021776

ISBN: 978-0-415-64354-2 (hbk)
ISBN: 978-0-415-64355-9 (pbk)
ISBN: 978-0-203-07900-3 (ebk)

Typeset in Bembo and Gill Sans
by Bookcraft Ltd, Stroud, Gloucestershire

Printed and bound in Great Britain by
TJ International Ltd, Padstow, Cornwall

The Beatles were wrong

Contents

List of figures

Acknowledgements

One of the most inspiring and practical books I have ever read on teaching is *Super Teaching* by the American educational pioneer Eric Jensen. It is from his original premise that there are seven elements needed for motivation in the classroom that I have chosen my seven keys as chapter titles, and then greatly expanded upon them.

I would also like to thank a number of people who have been significant in a number of ways in my own journey. My sincere thanks to Sue and Paul Chamberlain, Joan Ebsworth, Angela Preston, Andy Vass, Bill Cuthell, Margaret Abbott, Lis Howarth and her team, Margaret Holman and the Danger and Excitement Group, Mike and Pamela Cousins and the Raising Standards Partnership schools, Frank Robinson and all those who have had faith from the beginning and, now especially, Roy Leighton.

One omission from the original list of acknowledgements above is of course Alison Foyle and the team at Routledge who originally gave me the opportunity to write this book and now, with this revised version, the chance to put right that wrong. It is also an opportunity to thank Geoff Barton for his original review in the *Times Educational Supplement* that gave the book such a lift.

And, now, how can I not thank all those people around the world who have read this book and then told me – and, better still, told everyone else – how much it means to them. Thank you!*

---

* Or if you read the Spanish language version, *Motivar Para Aprender en el Aula*, gracias.

Preface to the second edition

A lot can happen over ten years in the world of education. When I was writing *Essential Motivation in the Classroom*, schools were under intense government pressure to improve, teacher morale was being constantly hammered by the Chief Inspector of Schools, the *Daily Mail* was proclaiming that exams were getting easier, everyone was complaining that standards were dropping, young people were becoming increasingly disenchanted with schools that seemed out of touch with their own reality and everyone was bemoaning the state of classroom behaviour and motivation. Now, ten years on, er ... .

Anyway, apart from the relentless drive for school improvement, teacher morale, educational standards, doubts over exam rigour, classroom relevance, student behaviour and the *Daily Mail*, so much has changed in the last decade. For a start, as Homer Simpson once said, 'They have the Internet on computers now'. When I was first writing this book, a computer was a computer, a phone was a phone, a camera was a camera, a portable music player was a Walkman and if you put all four on the table in front of you, you knew which was which. The OECD was something to do with economics, PISA was a tower, Hackney Downs was a failing school in north London, Local Education Authorities had at least some authority over local education and Bluetooth was a little-known tenth century Danish king. And wifi, iPads, Wikipedia and Twitter were twinkles in the eyes of some very clever

people who had a view that things could be better and technology could do something about it.

Despite the changes that have taken place in the world of
learning – and underpinning the things that have remained the
same – people are people, teachers are teachers, children are children and politicians are what they always have been and always
will be: which might explain the popularity of this book and
why we are updating it for its tenth anniversary. What I tried
to get across as I was writing it the first time around was not a
series of tricks and tips for coercing young people into learning
but a multi-faceted understanding of what was at the heart of
the sort of internal motivation that would lead to young people
actually wanting to learn for themselves. This is the essence of
essential motivation.

While I was very proud of this book, and remain so, the
enthusiasm with which it was greeted took me by surprise. I had
simply set out to write the book that no one else could have and,
as well as producing a book that I am pleased to have written,
I seem to have produced a book that many thousands of people
are pleased to have read. Which means that all I have done with
this revision is to tweak it here and there, to alter a few references that are no longer valid, to update elements of the science
where the science has been updated, to change a few names that
no longer resonate (or add the prefix 'the late' to too many of the
names for my liking) and to give it a little spruce up for its tenth
anniversary edition.

In doing so I hope that it will long continue to be a source of
inspiration and advice for educationalists everywhere when it
comes to bringing the best out of learners and helping them to
discover what is the very essence of motivation in the classroom.

Ian Gilbert
Santiago, May 2012

How to read this book

> Every idea in this book may turn out to be wrong, but
> that would be progress.
>
> Steven Pinker, *How the Mind Works*

With all that is going on in schools today there is a need for a
profound, academic and theoretical book on motivation in the
classroom. This is not it.

I am not a neuroscientist, a pedagogical theorist or an
academic researcher, although I know some people who are.
I do not write this book from any point of view other than as
someone who knows things that can – and do – make a real
and genuine difference in a classroom full of living, breathing
people.

Over the last few years I have soaked up information about
learning like a sponge. This book is me wringing myself out.
There are items of research that I have picked up for which I do
not know the source, I'm afraid. Yet, if I quote it here, I present
it in good faith and know it to be valid because it works in practice. And, anyway, I do not want to encumber either of us with
vast footnotes* and appendices. I simply want you to read this

---

* A footnote to my explanation why there are no footnotes. This
book was written in a time before Wikipedia, before Diigo, before
Pinterest, before Twitter, before all manner of social media making

book quickly and easily and enjoy the process. This work is also relevant for all teachers at any level and so, for reasons of inclusion, I interchange 'learner' with 'child' with 'student'.

I have also peppered the pages of this book with the words of men and women wiser than I, so feel free to use them for posters, assemblies, newsletters and thoughts for the week (or thoughts for the day if you do not feel you can hold a thought that long). Many use the term 'man', 'men' or 'he' when actually they refer to humans generally, so please excuse the anachronism. Be aware that I also draw upon an evolutionist frame of reference rather than a creationist one.

While I want you to walk away from this book and be able to take ideas straight into the classroom for immediate effect, I have not set it out as a step-by-step guide. Motivation is more than just a set of prescriptions; you will also need to reflect deeply on what teaching and learning is all about. This will be especially true as you consider the changes needed to take the 'teaching school' model and turn it inside out and upside down to create a 'learning school'.

'We know that teaching does not simply produce learning.'

Professor John MacBeath, during his time on the government's Taskforce for Education, giving an indication why he probably never received a Christmas card from one-time Ofsted chief, the teaching-centric Sir Chris Woodhead.

Be honest, not everything you teach is learned. We can teach for a week without anybody learning anything. I want this book to help you as you make the shift from teaching to learning, with all the positive effects on motivation – theirs and yours – that such a move brings. I have met too many teachers now who

---

it easy to source, store and share the very latest in research at the click of a button. Any research I do allude to here you can find for yourself with a quick online search now so please do. But watch out for the research that tells you that those things you do in your classroom that work, don't.

have said things like, 'I've been teaching for more than thirty years and I've never enjoyed it as much as I do now', 'I feel like I've been teaching asleep for the past ten years' or 'I've never felt as alive in the classroom as I have over the last few months.' These are all genuine quotes from real teachers, the last from a woman who said she had been teaching since 1965.

> 'If you're not learning, I'm just talking.'
>
> Slogan seen on a teeshirt – sometimes it takes an item of clothing to help us see the truth.

Furthermore, I have seen too many instances of children who re-find their fire for learning as a result of the changes that the teacher has made, sometimes without even being aware of it. A teacher recently told me how he had pointed out to one of his year 11 students how she had got herself back on track again after a poor time the previous year. When he commented that she had changed she said abruptly, 'No, Sir, you've changed!'

Too often in the classroom, and within the disciplinary systems in a school, it is the symptoms that are being treated – the poor behaviour, the lack of motivation, the disaffection – rather than the causes. Young people act the way they do for a reason that is in their self-serving interest. How can we ensure that we are not so busy looking at the acts that we overlook the reasons? When those children misbehave, why do they do that? Asking why until you dig deep enough is a powerful management technique that takes no prisoners. A headteacher once told me how he used it with his staff: 'This class isn't achieving the results they are capable of, Headteacher!' – 'Why are they not achieving those results, Miss Jones?' – 'Because they are too busy messing around.' – 'Why are they messing around?' – 'Because they are bored.' – 'Why are they bored?' – 'Oh, is that the bell … ?'.

> 'To teach (someone) a lesson: to cause (someone) to suffer the unpleasant consequences of some behaviour or action.'
>
> *Oxford English Dictionary* – so it must be true.

Although every teacher needs to have a range of powerful and effective behaviour management techniques *and* be backed up by a school-wide system that lets everybody know where they stand, this alone is not enough. Addressing the *causes* of the symptoms can – and does – prevent many discipline problems arising. Yes, many factors contribute to the mindsets of children as they walk into school in the morning. Yet, above all else, it is what you do that will be the deciding factor in the quality of the learning experience for all of you. And I do not say that to blame you, or to bash you, but to empower you. You do have the control and influence necessary to make a difference. *The Elton Report* from 1989 concluded that 'the behaviour of the teacher is the single most important factor that determines student behaviour'. And according to accelerated learning pioneer Dr Georgi Lozanov there is even a name for the 'sickness caused by poor teaching methods' – didactogenic syndrome.

'The history of the world shows that methods of political action that are used by the oppressed are determined by the oppressor.'

Nelson Mandela on where to start the search for ways to address motivation and behaviour.

Think in terms of: 'Can't Learn; Won't Learn'. Some can but won't; others would if they could but feel they can't. To address motivation we need to look at both to ensure the 'can'ts' can and the 'won'ts' will. This means we cannot separate learning strategies from motivation to learn and also that we look beyond mere strategies to the feel for motivation at an attitudinal level. *This is the essence of the 'essential motivation' in the title*. And that means *your* motivation as well as theirs; after all, the way that you are in the classroom teaches far louder than what you say.

No printed word, nor spoken plea
Can teach young minds what they should be

Not all the books on all the shelves
But what the teachers are themselves

Another stanza from the great poet Anon.

Some of the ideas I suggest will not work all of the time, but all of them will work some of the time. Above all, the book is designed to give you insights, ideas, support and succour as you do what you need to do to make the changes in your classroom that will lead to better motivation and learning and a far more fulfilling experience for everyone. Read it with a highlighter pen in one hand, a pen in the other for your own ideas, an open mind and a song in your heart. (Choose any three from the above.) And then, when you have read it, go and *do* something:

'If we come here today and there's no trouble tomorrow then we haven't done our jobs.'

Gloria Steinham

Introduction

> Everything has been said already but as no-one listens one
> must always start again.
>
> André Gide

You are a great teacher. You know it. Your colleagues know
it, although of course they do not let on – professional jealousy
and all that. Your line manager knows it. Even the parents
know it. Why, then, do your students not know it? They sit
there like puddings, passive and inert, while you show how
great a teacher you are with your pyrotechnic displays of
knowledge and wit. If only they were better motivated, they
would appreciate how good you really are and results would
really start to rocket.

Motivation is one of the most-used words in teaching today,
usually in the phrase, 'How can I motivate these kids?' It is
also a very misunderstood process. That question alone reveals
that we are approaching motivation from the wrong angle:
'carrot and stick' may work if you want a classroom full of
donkeys, but real motivation comes from within. Napoleon
may have said that men will die for ribbons, but his successes
were short-lived.

One of the *Harvard Business Review*'s most requested arti-
cles is one first published in 1968 by Professor Frederick

Herzberg, entitled 'One more time – how do you motivate employees?'. Here the professor talks about KITA – 'Kick In The Ass' – motivation. It gets the job done but does not lead to better-motivated employees. He describes the training of his one-year-old Schnauzer puppy; when it was little, if he kicked it, it would move ('push motivation'). After obedience training, he could offer the dog a biscuit and it would move ('pull motivation'). Yet on neither occasion was it the dog who was motivated to move. As the professor points out: 'the dog wants the biscuit, but it is I who want it to move'. Perhaps a better question for our staffrooms is: 'How can I get these kids to motivate themselves?'

In this book I want to offer practising teachers – and let's face it, we all need the practice – a range of strategies, some ideas and insights to help them consider what they can do to have better-motivated children in their classrooms.

There are no magic wands and it will take effort. You may even have to change the way that you do things; as the great actor once said, 'Where's my motivation?' For example, a professor of education once described how when he was in teacher training in the 1970s he used to instruct the student teachers to 'play to the intellect and then the emotional brain will follow'. He now knows that is totally back to front, that we have to play to the emotional brain; then, and only then, will we open up the intellectual brain (see Chapter 6 for more details). And Professor Tim Brighouse describes how he used to tell teachers that there were three things going on at any given time in a classroom: 'children taking new information on board, children processing the new information, children being entertained, having fun'. The last one, he now knows, has to be an integral part of the first two for them to be effective. If such high-profile figures are prepared to admit to changing their minds, are you? ('Change your mind, prove you've got one, that's what I say,' as Jools Holland once declared.)

Learning was once described as a four-step process – UI, CI, CC, UC – as follows:

Step 1: unconscious incompetence

This is when you don't know that you don't know. For example, at the age of six you don't know that you don't know how to drive a car.

Step 2: conscious incompetence

Now you are sitting in the car for the first time and suddenly realise how stupid you are as you look at all the mirrors, dials, levers and pedals (three pedals and only two feet?). You are now starting the learning process and becoming aware of all those skills that you never knew you did not have. This is where you need the motivation to kick in. Do you face up to your own stupidity and progress to step 3, or do you retreat backwards up the dead end of your own ignorance?

Step 3: conscious competence

As you learn new habits, to begin with you have to think hard about what you are doing in order to accomplish them. Not yet second nature, new skills seem hard, and part of your brain screams, 'I'll never be able to do this!' as you get out and slam the door at the traffic lights, leaving your father in the passenger seat looking apologetically at the truck driver behind you, who has now missed the green light for the fourth time.

Step 4: unconscious competence

'This is easy!' New skills no longer need conscious processing and are as easy to you as tying a shoelace or getting a soufflé to rise, or even both together with real practice. Have you ever turned up at school when you meant to go to the supermarket?

The need for motivation is as vital in steps 2 and 3 for you, as a learning professional, as it is for your students. Do *you* know how stupid you are? More importantly, are you prepared to accept it and *do something about it*? Indeed, some are pushing for a fifth step in this process now, with contenders being 'complacency' (what the inspectors like to call 'coasting' these days, where you are so busy being good at what you do you fail to notice that you could – and should – actually be better) and 'conscious competence of unconscious incompetence' or being aware of the fact that there are things you don't know you're not any good at yet. This moves us into Donald Rumsfeld's world of known and unknown knowns and unknowns, and should be treated with caution. Suffice to say, motivation is important both to get better and then to keep on getting better.

As teachers, we spend a great deal of time knowing all the answers. To a certain extent, that is our job, or at least it used to be. In many ways the system – notably beyond primary-school age – called for a collection of professional 'know-it-alls', paid to share what they had picked up at university with the community at large. That was then.

> 'How can we remember our ignorance, which our growth requires, if we are using our knowledge all the time?'
>
> Thoreau on why, as teachers, we need to be learners too. Ever heard the joke about the teacher who dreamt he was giving a lesson and then woke to find that he was?

Now we are experiencing the democratisation of knowledge on a huge scale. My youngest daughter has access to all the knowledge in the world at her fingertips. And it is updated daily. No human could compete with that, and nor should we want to. Microsoft weren't the first to talk about 'the guide from the side not the sage on the stage'. There is a tremendously powerful role for educators in the great new era, not as founts of all knowledge, but as pioneers in the democratisation of learning. Helping young people want to acquire new knowledge (the motivation part), helping them know where to find it, how to know good knowledge from bad, how to know what to do with it when they find it – this is the stuff of the educator's role in the twenty-first century. Are you up for it? Are you motivated to do something about it? Are you prepared to accept your own ignorance as the starting point for this journey?

Please approach this book with a demeanour of curious stupidity. As Lao wrote, 'To know that you do not know is best. To not know of knowing is a disease'. Once you become aware of your own stupidity and (re)start your own personal journey with your own motivational engines firing, you have a chance. We all have. After all, society needs great educators. Society needs you to be brilliant. The future of the world is depending on it.

Chapter 1

Motivated for what?

Bad news, I'm afraid. The culmination of six million years' worth of neurological evolution is not the GCSE.

The human brain is the product of millions upon millions of adaptations and changes, which ensures that we are the ones best able to cope with what life will throw at us. And I am sorry to say that a key stage 2 SAT or a French vocabulary test is not among the eventualities that natural selection has prepared us for. Perhaps if the consequences of not having done your homework had been far more stringent hundreds of thousands of years ago, this might not be the case, but it is.

In a fascinating book, modestly entitled *How the Mind Works*, Stephen Pinker suggests: 'Without an understanding of what the brain was designed to do in the environment in which we evolved the unnatural activity called education is unlikely to succeed.'

At the end of the day the brain is designed for one thing – survival. It does all sorts of other wonderful things, some of which we can barely begin to imagine, but the bottom line is that it is there to keep us and our progeny going. What this means is that each year millions of young people are tested for their ability to do something unnatural and biologically inconsequential. And if they fail to measure up, the implication is that something is wrong with them. As British business guru and troubleshooter the late Sir John Harvey Jones noted: 'We have an education system that is designed to get 200,000 children a year or so into university. Everybody who doesn't make it to university is told at some point that they have failed.'

As we approach a learning situation, there is a part of our brain that pops the question: 'Do I need this learning in order to survive? Yes or no?' If yes, then we can get on with the learning in hand and start to tap into our potential. However, if the answer is no, forget it.

> 'The brain's main function is to keep the organism of which it is a part alive and reproducing. All other tricks ... arise out of that single overriding ambition.'
>
> Neuroscientist Rita Carter, in *Mapping the Mind*, explaining why we sometimes have trouble remembering the French for how to get to the ironmongers.

Do those children for whom school learning is a write-off know their drugs, their darts scores, the safest way home, how to ride a skateboard, hot-wire a car, memorise computer game 'cheats', assess risk and reward, understand the needs of plants, care for and train dogs, motivate others, be part of, or even lead, a team?

In Chapter 2 we will look at our latest understanding of the nature of intelligence and how we are finally learning to be more intelligent about intelligence. One of the most liberating insights here is multiple intelligence theory – the idea that we have at least eight different intelligence areas to draw on, and that our IQ-based society has taken far too narrow and exclusionist a view about the nature of smartness. For example, one of the intelligences identified is 'naturalistic intelligence', exhibited by vets, RSPCA inspectors, farmers, zoologists and the like. In the 'This Land' countryside section of the *Financial Times* weekend supplement there was once this description of a young rural resident, written by the correspondent Roger Scruton.

> Vince is 14 years old, an inveterate truant who has now been excluded from our local school, to which he reacted

as you and I would react to false imprisonment. He cannot read or write, and lives with his equally illiterate parents in a cottage by the railway ... Visits from the school inspector and the social worker notwithstanding Vince is content with his lot. Moreover unlike the majority of teenage boys in our local school, he has a clear vision of his future career, and skills that amply fit him to pursue it. For Vince wants to be a pest control officer. He identifies instinctively with wild animals ... He knows their habits and their habitats, how to capture them, care for them and also kill them ... He has a menagerie of birds and rodents, including four barn owls which he has bred himself, a pair of ferrets, and a collection of lurchers and terriers ... He can coax owls and hawks into any territory and provide them with a nesting place.

Financial Times, 28 October 2000

The message seems quite clear – don't tell me that Vince is an unmotivated, incapable learner. Scruton goes on to suggest that school was not Vince's thing because 'his soul was not shaped to pass through such a mill'. What, then, is the 'shape of the soul' of these seemingly unmotivated young boys and girls sitting before you? Once we know that, we can start to open the door of true motivation.

The whole notion of the brain being designed for survival has been summed up, somewhere down the accelerated learning timeline, in the neat phrase 'What's in it for me?', known affectionately as the WIIFM? and pronounced 'wiff-im'. As children enter your classroom the question is always the same: What's in it for me? What is the point? Why should I bother learning this? Often the phrase is unspoken. It simply lies there in the background, subtly undermining our meticulously thought-out attempts to make the lesson moderately enjoyable. The extent to which the cries of 'What's the point?' and 'Do we have to?' are vocalised, or just kept beneath the surface, depends on the subject being covered. Ask a languages teacher.

A Young Man's Epigram on Existence

A senseless school, where we must give
Our lives that we may learn to live!
A dolt is he who memorizes
Lessons that leave no time for prizes

A twenty-six-year-old Thomas Hardy discovering the WIIFM? for himself in 1866.

We spend a great deal of time teaching young people the *how to*, but we need to ensure that the *why* is addressed before we even approach the *how to*. There are big WIIFM?s that deal with the purpose of our life and there are smaller ones to do with our immediate needs, so let's start small.

An activity I ask teachers to do during my INSET sessions is a WIIFM? exercise. In faculty or department groups – or year groups in primary schools – I ask them to take ten minutes to discuss the WIIFM?s for a particular subject or topic area from the point of view of the learners. What *is* in it for them? How will they *benefit* from learning what you are trying to teach them? Notice the use of the word 'benefit'. A good salesperson will always talk in terms of 'benefits' rather than 'features', so make sure you do the same. 'Global awareness', for example, is a feature. If you are not sure whether you have identified a benefit or a feature, try putting 'So what?' on the end. If you don't, the children will. 'Which means that … ' is another way of ensuring you are dealing in benefits.

Marketing your subject

One of the things I recommend to individual departments is some sort of marketing campaign to raise awareness of the need for success in a particular subject area. This, for example, is often the case with languages, as so many people, from the parents to fellow colleagues, may well believe that there is no need to learn a foreign language because 'everybody speaks English, don't they?' A head of maths I met recently was telling me how he was working to get a 'buzz' back around his subject. Is there a 'buzz' where you work? If so, how do you do it? Tell others in your school. If not, what could you do so that others will come to you wanting what you have to offer? Pay attention to the environment in which you are going to 'market' your subject. I have noticed posters in libraries featuring personalities engaged in reading (footballers studying books without pictures, that sort of thing), encouraging young people to do the same. Advertising reading in the library is like advertising beer in a pub. Make sure your message is positioned where the need is rather than at the point of the solution.

Put your WIIFM?s up on the walls of your classroom. Look out for them in your day-to-day life. Here are three I have found on my travels:

> **Arithmetic stirs up him who is by nature sleepy and dull and makes him quick to learn and shrewd (Plato on maths)**

> **The further back you look, the further forward you are likely to see (Churchill on history)**

> **Studying English literature at school was my first step towards mental freedom and independence. It was like falling in love with life (novelist Ian McEwan on English)**

Once you have looked at this through the learners' eyes, go and actually ask the learners themselves. They might come up with things you had not thought of. In the middle of Birmingham I once led such an activity with a group of sixth-formers at a Catholic girls' school. One group was from very traditional Muslim families and were wearing the traditional attire rather than the school uniform. These girls were all doing A-level geography, and when asked to write down their WIIFM?s had written 'field trips', and then in brackets 'independence'. I found out later that these girls were dropped off outside the school gates every morning by a family member and picked up again at 3.30 p.m. They never had the chance to go anywhere on their own, but the A-level geography field trip would change all that.

How to jump the queue for the photocopier

Research has shown that when a person asks to enter the queue ahead of a colleague and can come up with a reason why, the colleague will let them in ('no why, no way!')

One science teacher I know spends the first four lessons of her year 7 course on the WIIFM?s for science, asking the students what they think science will help them with. They then do some poster work to create a 'WIIFM? wall'. The benefits her students came up with included the fact that science would help them when they go to the doctor, with their gardening, even with their cooking.

The following is a genuine piece of tutorial work from what, if I recall properly, was a year 10 boy at a school in Carlisle. The staff of the religious studies Department called me over while they were doing the WIIFM? exercise and showed me this passionately handwritten piece which would bring a tear to the eye of any religious studies teacher. He had written:

> Some of my compulsory reports were not as I had hoped but I get easily distracted by my peers! I must work on my concentration. However, I have done reasonably well on

the subjects that MATTER and are RELEVANT TO LIFE like RS [religious studies].

Who cares about π and finding x and that (**!&@@**!!!) Pythagoras?

At least in RS we can talk about the world and the terrible state it is in. We were told in PSE that science answers HOW, but RS answers WHY. It doesn't take an Einstein to work out which is the more important. Stuff all the Maths and science and English (*@@&!!*&@!!!) and start dealing with

PEOPLE

The world is in a mess and we are all busting a gut about triangles, diffusion and the works of Shakespeare. Is this going to feed the homeless – NO! Is this going to stop famine – NO!

Is this going to stop war and violence?

NO! NO! NO!

You may not agree with that child (unless you are an RS teacher), but that doesn't matter; although given the state of the world currently he may well be right. By understanding where a child is coming from you can use his or her natural motivation and creatively adapt it to your own subject. I have yet to meet a child who isn't motivated; sometimes they just aren't motivated to do what we want them to do when we want them to do it.

'Do not train boys to learn by force and harshness but lead them by what arouses them so that you may better understand the bent of their minds'

Plato on the boon Megan Fox can be in your lessons.

By getting to the core of their own WIIFM?s you start to get closer to the holy grail of the world of motivation – internal, or intrinsic, motivation.

I have heard countless tales told by parents, as well as teachers, of young people who seemed unmotivated, even incapable of learning, until the WIIFM? light was switched on in their heads. For example, some parents were telling me about their child who appeared to be having real trouble reading, until, that is, he went to his school's nativity in the local church and realised that he was the only one not able to read the words of the song from the projector screen. From that day on, he sorted out his reading, and the following year he was up at the lectern reading one of the Bible lessons.

'Desire must come from within, not as a result of being driven by coaches or teachers.'

Former Arsenal manager George Graham on how great football teams are driven in, but not by, coaches.

A headteacher told me about his son who hated reading but loved maths. One day he came home from school in tears (the son, that is, not the head) and, when asked why, explained that he had been put down to the second group for maths because he was unable to read the questions and was slowing down the group. From then on, the boy sorted out his reading because now there was 'a point'. And there was the teacher with a girl in her tutor group who was coasting through history in an under-achieving manner until she spotted some classroom WIIFM? posters about the 'whys' for history and realised that it would help her achieve her goal of being a barrister. Now, according to her teacher, she is coasting through history in a high-achieving manner.

To demonstrate the power of the 'why', try this experiment with your students. Find one who is confident of not achieving an A grade in, say, English GCSE. Then suggest this deal to them:

'Will you get an A grade in GCSE English if I agree to give you one million pounds for doing it?'

My experience is, nine times out of ten, the student will immediately agree (although sometimes they push me as far as £1,750,000). When asked what has caused the change of heart, the reply usually comes in a sheepish manner: 'The money'. A reply I once heard was: 'There's a reason now'. The implication here, of course, is that there was no reason before. And we wonder why they are not switched on. To go on to point out to them that they are capable of achieving things that money cannot buy, let alone a mere million pounds, if – and only if – they start to tap into what they have to offer, is quite a powerful exercise.

> 'I told myself I had to know what I was going to do with my life or I would be lost.'
>
> Fashion designer Stella McCartney showed that, even at the age of 13, all you need is goal-setting (and that there's more to success than having a rich father).

What is their 'why'? Where do they want to go? What do they want to do? Who do they want to be? How is what they are doing daily at school going to help them get there? Help them to have an inspiring enough 'why' – a major defining purpose – to get them out of bed in the morning. They are very relevant questions for sixteen-year-olds, of course, but still powerful with young children. After all, research shows that 60 per cent of all working scientists developed an interest in their field by the age of 11. Even if the 'why' changes, it doesn't matter. Having a 'why' is more important than hitting the 'why.'

The film *Stand and Deliver* is the true story of maths teacher Jaime Escalante working with Latino students from the wrong side of the Los Angeles tracks. He helped them all achieve unprecedented levels of success in their advanced placement tests in calculus, so much so that the education board assumed they must have cheated and made everyone resit. When they passed again and the board hauled up Escalante before them to explain how he had done it, he offered one word of explanation: *ganas*, Spanish for 'desire'.

Another exercise that helps to hit this point home is to ask children to write the following two sentences. The first one starts 'I am … ' and should be completed with what they hope to be doing in one or two years' time, ideally after having taken their GCSEs. For example, they may write:

> I am in St Cuthbert's VIth form studying A level English, French and Art.

> I am working for Browns and doing a BTEC in engineering.

Notice how these sentences use the three Ps of effective goal-setting affirmations – personal, present tense and a positive; that is, what you want and not what you don't want.

To make the sentences even more powerful, ask them to write this underneath:

> To get there I got …

Then instruct them to write down the subjects they are currently studying, along with the grades, that will take them to the next stage in their lives. Recommend to them that they take these sentences and stick them up somewhere where they can see them daily, for example at the desk where they revise, or keep them in a diary or in a wallet – anywhere where they see them regularly. Focusing daily on your goals is an important part of the goal-setting process. Writing them down on New Year's Eve and putting them away until the following year is not. Tiger Woods had the top scores of Jack Nicklaus taped to the inside of his wardrobe door as he was growing up so that every day he could see what he had to do to achieve his goal of being better than his hero.

And while you have them in this goal-focused mode, ask them to turn to the person sitting next to them and say in a firm but slightly patronising manner:

'Don't just pack for the airport, will you!'

School is not a destination – it is simply an extended packing process. Students should be leaving with their bags crammed with the skills and knowledge (in that order) necessary to take their places successfully in the twenty-first century. Remind them of that – if they are coasting towards D grades in their GCSEs because that is all they need to get into college, they are selling themselves short.

To encourage young people to work in that goal-focused way is one of the most important success skills you can impart and will last them a very active and rewarding lifetime. And remember the importance of 'walking the talk'. You should be doing it too. After all, it is natural. Pinker cites computer scientists Allen Newell and Herbert Simon's definition of intelligence as 'specifying a goal, assessing the current situation to see how it differs from the goal, and applying a set of operations to reduce the difference'. Goal-setting and intelligence, then, are inter-related. You want to be intelligent? Then set goals. As Pinker suggests: 'Without goals the very concept of intelligence is meaningless.'

What, then, are the goals of the young people you are working with? By understanding the process of effective goal setting, teaching and modelling it to your students and then encouraging them to use their goals to link into the WIIFM?s in the lessons, you are really starting to tap into the core of their internal motivation as well as teaching them what is the key success tool.

Goal-setting made simple

Step 1 What do you want?
Be specific. 'I want to go abroad' is not very specific. Abroad is a big place.

Step 2 When do you want it?
A goal without a deadline is a wish. But give a wish a deadline …

Step 3 Start
The journey of a thousand miles begins with a small step (or a flat tyre).

Step 4 Check and re-check
Is what I am doing taking me where I want to be going? If yes, keep on keeping on. If no, do what you need to do to get back on course.

Step 5 Enjoy the journey

As Cervantes said, 'The road is better than the inn'.

I am aware that the average person in the UK quite often meets any talk of goal-setting with one of two reactions. It is either, 'oh no, not more of that happy-clappy, positive-thinking, trans-Atlantic psychobabble' or, alternatively, 'oh no, not more of that boring, rigid, SMART-based, time-consuming mumbo-jumbo'.

Perhaps the key word in the above paragraph is the word 'average'. I have not come across an individual doing extraordinary things in any walk of life who did not use goal setting, in some form or another, to achieve what he or she had achieved and were not still using it to go on achieving. It is, without doubt, the ultimate success process and seems to tie in so well with the brain's natural propensity towards being what is known as a 'goal-seeking organism'.

'My first car was a Mini Metro … it was a good car, it got me from A to B. But nowadays I want to go to C.'

Champion boxer Prince Naseem talking metaphorically – and literally – on what you achieve with high expectations and a clear destination.

There is the story, regularly rolled out to confirm the power of goal setting, regarding the survey of students at Yale University in the 1930s. In among a whole host of questions designed to draw a picture of the young, upwardly-mobile American of the time, was a question asking the respondent whether he or she had *written* goals with plans for their achievement. (Writing them down is important, as founder of Domino Pizzas, Tom Monaghan, says from his own experience, 'It's the thinking that goes into the writing, not the words that end up on the paper, that makes the difference'.) Only a handful did. Thirty years later, so the story goes, the University followed up to see just what they had achieved. What they discovered was that students who had written goals were all happy and successful in a number of ways, were all financially independent and were all worth more individually than the rest of the students put together.

Apocryphal or not, the principle behind the story has held true in so many cases. We bring more out of ourselves when we know where we are going and commit to at least the first few steps towards getting there.

'As long as you're going to think anyway – you might as well think BIG.'

Donald Trump on goals, buildings, ego and hair.

As for the nature of the goals, the last thing you want is 'achievable' and 'realistic' goals for yourself (the A and the R of the SMART goal-setting process). That said, 'specific' is fine, as are 'measurable' and 'time-based' (the S, M and T of SMART respectively). Please rip out this page of the book and stick up the following sentence:

Nobody achieved their full potential aiming for the obvious.

'The secret of life is to have a task. Something that you devote your entire life to, something to bring everything to, every minute of the day, for your whole life. And the most important thing is, it must be something you can't possibly do.'

Henry Moore, the sculptor, on the meaning of life and how being a teacher means you're halfway there anyway.

As we look at the WIIFM? from the bigger perspective, may I take this opportunity of welcoming you to the 'Anything Possible World'. I do not know what you know about the state of the world of work currently, but I am aware that there is no expectation for a teacher to have his or her finger on the pulse of twenty-first-century working life. Yet I believe such an understanding is crucial to your efficacy at preparing young people for the road ahead of them. If we are ignorant ourselves of what lies beyond school, how can we adequately prepare them for it, beyond filling them with clichés and anachronisms? Preparing young people to succeed in a world of which you have no experience is like me as a French teacher preparing young people for a trip to Paris without ever having been there myself. I can do it, but can I do it well enough? Could I do it better? Do my students deserve more?

Let me give you some examples. Did you know that you have more computer technology in a singing birthday card than existed in the entire world before 1950; that a mobile telephone has more computer power than was used in the first ever space launch; that the on-board computer in a top-of-the-range Mercedes has more computer power than had the on-board computer in the first space shuttle; that through nanotechnology we can build machines that are so small you can barely see them; that by a process called personal fabrication we can download things like watches and print them out; that we are already trialling a heat-seeking submarine which is just 4mm long, to deliver medicines, lasers and cameras into the bloodstream; or that if you wanted to buy bullet-proof glass for your office through which you could fire out but no one could fire in, you could? (Just make sure you put it in the right way around.)

Does this describe a world of work that you recognise? On the one hand, the speed of change is frightening, while on the other we are living in hugely exciting times with tremendous possibilities out there for those who know how to make the most of them. Are the children leaving your school passionately excited about the future? And are they creative enough to grasp the opportunities on offer? An exercise I do with children, both of primary age and at secondary level, is to give them three minutes, working in pairs, to describe a world where anything is possible. After all, the future of the world is not out there. That is the present. The future lies between their ears.

> 'The future will be better tomorrow.'
>
> George W. Bush, in whose hands our futures once lay.

With young children, as you might expect, such an exercise throws up all sorts of wonderful ideas and inventions (self-peeling bananas, chocolate bars that get bigger the more you eat, cars that do your hair and put on your make-up as you drive to work). For the older children – and, I must say, some of the brighter young children – such an exercise is always a more sober affair, with most groups not really making it past world peace and flying cars. (Although flying cars are not to be sniffed at. A friend of mine, who can only be referred to as a cheese millionaire, was convinced that the future of personal transport will be personal flight. People might consider that a little mad but then that is what they said about Bill Gates when he declared that he would like to see 'a computer on every desk and in every home throughout the land'. It is obvious now, but it was not so long ago that experts, for example those in a 1947 engineering magazine, were predicting that 'computers of the future would weigh no less than one and a half tons'!)

In *Fortune* magazine recently, Paul Allen, who was Bill Gates's partner in the early years of the Microsoft story and is still hugely influential in business and technology, said

> Science has opened the door but artistry and creativity will take us through it.

Are the children leaving your school passionate about the future and wildly creative and imaginative, with the belief that, say, they are entering a world where anything is possible, that they have the world's most powerful piece of equipment between their ears, and that if they can imagine it they can do it?

> **'If you're looking ahead long term and what you see looks like science fiction it might be wrong. But if it doesn't look like science fiction it's definitely wrong.'**
>
> **Futurologist and co-author of *Next: Trends for the Near Future* Marian Salzman, on why we shouldn't scoff at self-peeling bananas.**

The world is full of material that we take for granted today but which someone, somewhere, was once told was impossible. Roger Bannister was told that if he ran that fast, his heart would burst. Chuck Yeager was told that if he tried to fly through the sound barrier, the vibrations would lead to the disintegration of his craft. In 1865 the *Boston Post* declared that: 'Well informed people know that it is impossible to transmit the voice over wires and that were it possible to do so, the thing would be of no practical value.' I find no record of the reliability of the tips on their racing pages. Aerodynamically speaking, bees cannot fly. It's just that they don't know it. Scientifically speaking, a pike should not be able to accelerate as fast as a NASA rocket, which is at twelve times the force of gravity. So, don't tell it.

> **'The human spirit is indomitable. No one can ever say you must not run faster than this or jump higher than that.**

> There will never be a time when the human spirit will not be able to better existing records.'
>
> Roger Bannister on why we should always look forward to the Olympics.

A deputy head in Newcastle-upon-Tyne told one of his students to 'pull the other one' when he said that he wanted to be a footballer; the same deputy told another guitar-playing student that he would 'never get anywhere playing that kind of stuff'. Fortunately, both Shearer and Knopfler (for it was they) had the presence of mind to go for their goals. So did Buddy Holly ('The biggest no talent I have ever worked with'), Fred Astaire ('Can't act. Can't sing. Can dance a little'), Ronald Reagan ('He doesn't have the Presidential look'), Clint Eastwood ('You have a chip on your tooth, your Adam's apple sticks out too far and you talk too slow'), Elvis Presley ('You ought to go back to driving a truck'), Marilyn Monroe ('You'd better learn secretarial skills or else get married'), not to mention Emily Brontë ('Will never be generally read', on *Wuthering Heights*) and Jane Austen ('We are willing to return the manuscript', on *Northanger Abbey*).

> 'He's totally unsuitable for English football'.
>
> With these words from former Everton FC manager Howard Kendall, Eric the King proceeded not to fit Eric Cantona to English football but to fit English football to Eric Cantona.

Want some more? Walt Disney was sacked from an advertising agency for having 'a singular lack of drawing ability'; Gary Cooper was rejected three times by the Performing Arts Society in his college before he went on to become an Oscar winner; Henry Ford almost went bankrupt on several occasions, as did Walt Disney (who had also been rejected by 302 banks before he had even started).

At this point, the non-believers usually chip in with a 'Yes, but …!' along the lines of: 'What about all those people who went for their goals but didn't make it?' Two things in reply:

1   There may be examples of individuals who have gone for their goals and not made it, but there can't be many examples of people who have not gone for their goals but still achieved. You can't win the lottery if you don't buy a ticket.

2   One of the biggest reasons people come up with for not encouraging young people to aim high is because, as one adviser put it to me, 'disappointment is a terrible thing'. Yet, surely the biggest disappointment any of us could ever face is that of arriving at the end of our lives to look back and realise that we never even really had a go. 'Twenty years from now you will be more disappointed by the things you didn't do, than by the things that you did do' as Mark Twain put it. *Surely, it is better to encourage young people to aim high and then give them strategies for coping with disappointment than to tell them never to try anything in case it doesn't work out?* That said, one of the ways of avoiding the Pollyanna nature of goal-setting is to make sure that step 4 in the 'Goal-setting made simple' box (p. 17) is done regularly, even daily. If you are constantly reviewing your course and your progress, there should be no surprise if you want to be a professional foot-baller but aren't even making third team. (As I pointed out to one teacher worried about how to dissuade students who wanted to play for the Arsenal football team, if every young person was dissuaded from such a dream there would be no Arsenal football team.)

'What you really regret was never asking the girl to dance.'

The late Steve Jobs on the real meaning of failure.

And, if you are looking to back up the principle of big goals in a Christian context, why not try Mark 11:23:

Whatever you ask for in prayer, believe you have received it, and it will be yours.

In a nutshell, how will we know what we are capable of unless we aim high enough – how high is high? And remember, this is aimed at you, the teacher, as much as at your charges in the classroom.

> 'We can so easily slip back from what we have struggled to attain, abruptly, into a life we never wanted; can find that we are trapped, as in a dream, and die there, without ever waking up.'
>
> German poet Rilke, on the great, imperceptible waste of our true potential.

One of the most powerful goal-setting exercises I have come across is contained in the following five questions. I have put these questions to thousands of young people and teachers in all sorts of schools in all sorts of places. I also answered them myself several years ago, and still have the notebook from 1990, over a decade before I did so, in which I wrote that 'I am a thinking skills expert in demand around the world' – note the use of the present tense and note that it works.

Please feel free to use them yourself and to put them to your learners, making sure they write their answers. Whatever you or they write is fine; there are no right or wrong answers. You do not have to share your answers with anyone, just answer each question honestly and fully.

The wish list

1   If the world were to end in twelve months, which five places would you visit before it did?
2   Somebody has invented a magic 'success' potion. Having taken the potion, no matter what you do, you will succeed. What five things would you do if you knew you could not fail?
3   It is International Work Experience Week, and you can try any job in the world. Which five would you try first?

4   You have been elected President of the World! What five
     things would you introduce to make the world a better
     place for everybody in it?
5   You have a magic pen. Whatever you write comes true.
     The magic only lasts for three minutes. Quickly write
     down your plans for the next five years. Include qualifica-
     tions, further education, year-off plans, hobbies you want to
     try, people you want to meet, places you want to go to, etc.

Your answers to the above questions are powerful indicators of
what your heart really wants, far more so than if I were to ask
you simply to write 'your goals', when we tend to write what is
safe or expected, or both. Without opening up the goal-setting
process to our creative side, we may never even realise just what
it is in life we are seeking.

One young teacher I met in a prep school in Surrey was joining
in with her students as they did the Wish List exercise. She was
from New Zealand and was travelling around the world via the
usual places – Europe, the Home Country, the US – yet, when she
answered the first question from the Wish List, she was shocked
to see she had written places such as the Antarctic and the North
Pole. Whose dreams was she living out? What about you?

One of the most startling of the right brain–left brain experiments I have come across was recounted by Rita Carter. She
tells the story of the young man who, for various neurological
reasons, had the link between the left and right hemispheres of
his brain severed. What made this man the subject of a great
deal of interest in neurological circles was the fact that his
right hemisphere was able to process a few phrases and words
– usually these are processed exclusively by the left. Because of
this anomaly, scientists had a rare occasion to communicate with
the right side of the brain – normally the non-verbal side and
the one traditionally associated with creativity – using language.
An elaborate experiment was devised whereby his left and right
hemispheres were asked questions independently of each other.
When asked about his future plans, the logical, sequential, feet-
on-the-ground, rational left brain stated that he was intending

to be a draftsman. However, when asked the same question, his right brain declared its intention to be an 'automobile racer'!

> 'We may all be carrying around in our skulls a mute prisoner with a personality, ambition and self-awareness quite distinct from the day-to-day entity we believe ourselves to be.'
>
> Rita Carter on how we might be someone we don't know we are.

In other words, when the logical constraints of SMART-type reasoning are taken away, another side of our personality starts to come through. And who is to say which is the 'real' one? Can you honestly tell the difference between fantasy and reality? After all, your brain can't. Research from Germany, which I came across some time ago, showed that, of the parts of the brain that are used when you play a sport, 70 per cent of those parts are used in thinking you are playing a sport. Huge parts of your brain do not know the difference between what you do and what you think you do. Even on just hearing the word 'screwdriver', parts of the motor cortex light up because of the historical associations we have with the word.

In the book *Mind Sculpture*, Ian Robertson describes an experiment in which a group of volunteers managed to increase their finger strength by 22 per cent just by visualising flexing their fingers, compared with a group that had actually been flexing their fingers which managed only 8 per cent more. You can be a couch potato and go for a jog at the same time, although, as Robertson points out, to do this you actually have to live the experience from within your body, as it were. You will not get fit just by watching yourself running up a hill.

When Danny is always misbehaving in a particular lesson and you become hoarse with your constant entreaties to behave, does Danny have a 'picture' in his head of what behaving looks like? If he does not, his brain does not know what it is expected to do; once he does, it can start working him towards it. 'What will Mr Jones say to you at the end of the week after you have had three brilliant lessons?' 'What will be the highlight of the week on this report card?' 'When I come in and see you learning wonderfully in Mrs Smith's lesson, what will you be doing?' By asking those sorts of questions you are beginning to implant in the child's brain a view of a different sort of reality.

> 'Cowardice … is almost always simply a lack of ability to suspend the functioning of the imagination.'
>
> Hemingway on FEAR – False Emotions Appearing Real (or, Forget Everything And Run, if you prefer). To overcome fears, see a reality where it is not the worst that happens, but the best. For example, see yourself delivering that brilliant speech, assembly or interview.

Another powerful visualising strategy is to say to the child: 'Close your eyes and tell me what this model volcano you are about to start working on will look like in three weeks' time when you have finished it.' One girl explained how she visualised her certificates with the grades that she wanted on them and had then even visualised herself into Cambridge! It was not all that she did, but it does show how such a process can start to open up our potential. After all, as the Austrian philosopher, American politician and action-hero Arnold Schwarzenegger says, 'If your brain can envisage the fact that you can do something, you can.'

> 'I used to get in trouble for dreaming … I would always visualise these things and the things that got me in trouble for dreaming are the things I am doing today … If you visualise it and see it clearly enough, in living colour, it's going to happen. As long as you're willing to work for it, it is going to happen. I really believe in that.'
>
> Lord of the Dance Michael Flatley on what you can achieve with a vision, effort and a stout pair of shoes.

I have three children. Don't tell them what they can or cannot do in a world where anything is possible. Teach them to aim high and develop strategies to cope with things not working out as planned but not this dread retreat from the possibility of disappointment. What chance do any of us have if we spend our lives avoiding possible defeat?

> 'Never tell a young person that something cannot be done. God may have been waiting for centuries for somebody ignorant enough of the impossible to do that thing.'
>
> American clergyman Dr J.A. Holme, on who we upset when we tell young people what they can or cannot do in the future.

Goal-setting is the key to internal motivation, yet it is so often extrinsic motivation that takes precedence at school. This is the motivation of carrots and sticks, kicking and cajoling, sanctions and rewards that so many of us employ just to drag children through the day. From your point of view, you receive an extrinsic reward for the work that you do: it is called money. We cannot live without it and it helps us achieve all sorts of personal goals. But is it rewarding in itself? A 1998 article in *Fortune* magazine summed it up: 'Financial incentives will get people to do more of what they are doing. Not better, just more.' Are you motivated to work because of the money? Does it bring you pleasure? If this is the case, each time you receive a pay increase you would also receive an increase in pleasure. Did your pleasure levels go up last year by 3.5 per cent, or whatever the national pay rise was? Did they stay there? If this was the case, the longer you had been in teaching the more ecstatic you would be (not the reverse), headteachers would be orgasmic for most of the day and as for the rest … 'I'm afraid the Director of Education can't leave his desk right now, his raise has just come through'!

> 'Forget the money, I want to beat the best.'
>
> Joe Calzaghe, WBO World Supermiddleweight Champion, on his internal motivation for hitting people in the face.

We know this not to be the case, however. Research shows that when we receive a pay increase our motivation rises temporarily but then returns to where it was before. Sustained motivation comes from somewhere other than our wallets.

Is there a place for external motivation in the classroom? Well, that depends upon our aims. If we are looking for any means possible to get young people through this or that hoop *regardless of the consequences*, then there can be. *Yet research has found that external motivation can inhibit intrinsic motivation.*

My daughter once brought a sunflower home from her primary school, which we looked after and protected, tying it to the trelliswork on the wall as it grew. We were amazed at how it grew: a thick, straight stem, almost 4cm in diameter, rising to a height of around 4m. We were both impressed with the result of our loving handiwork. A couple of weeks later we had a storm. In the morning we found the sunflower lying across the path like a felled tree. The tears went on for weeks until my daughter finally managed to get me to stop crying. Nearby, a pensioner had planted a veritable hedge of sunflowers that were neither staked nor tied to the wall and would flap about in the wind like a row of deliboppas in what I thought was a laughable way, yet after the storm all of these sunflowers were still standing.

> 'Ironically if people had given me a chance, I wouldn't have been so successful … It was because nobody thought I was capable of anything that I had to prove them wrong.'
>
> Michael Fraser, son of a Jamaican immigrant and the entrepreneur behind a £6.5 million aluminium import business, on what he learned by not being taught.

One of the experiences that seedlings have to go through is the process of being 'hardened', ready for life beyond the molly-coddling glass walls of the nursery. Without this, when they are finally faced with the ravages of wind, weather and incompetent gardeners, they would not survive.

'Winning does not tempt that man. This is how he grows: by being defeated, decisively, by constantly greater beings.'

The German poet Rilke with words of condolence relevant for the German goalkeeper in Munich on 1 September 2001.

Children need support and protection. They also need 'hardening', especially the high achievers in our classrooms, who do not know what failure is (of which more in Chapter 4). It is a notion best summed up in the favourite phrase of a deputy headteacher who was a pioneer when it came to helping her school become a learning school: 'Don't ride the bike for them.'

'The worst possible preparation for adulthood is to do well in your exams.'

Andrew McKie writing in the *Daily Telegraph*, adding that it's better to learn from an early age 'how to cope with failure' and to 'start as you mean to go on – by rejoicing in your 'F' grades in geography, physics or Greek'. And then apply for a job at the *Telegraph*.

The more we do for them, the less they will choose to do for themselves, creating a vicious cycle of learned helplessness. The more we push from the outside the less, ultimately, the child can do for itself from the inside. Are we crushing them – to give the system the benefit of the doubt – with kindness? Or, to be more cynical, are we focusing on short-term external factors simply to make the students, and hence the school, and hence the government of the day, look good?

'Nor do I believe in bombarding them with motivational stuff all the time. If you don't ration your interventions what you say evaporates.'

Manchester United's Alex Ferguson on why in teaching, as in many areas of life, less is more.

One headteacher I met realises now what had gone wrong with a group of students she had a year or so ago. It was an all-boy English GCSE group; nonetheless the class and the head worked very hard, and at their mock exams the boys were achieving better than she had thought possible. However, when it came to exam leave the boys took off and their motivation went quickly downhill. Those who did bother to turn up to their actual exams had done little revision, and few turned up with the texts and equipment to succeed. They nearly all failed. Who was the one motivated for them to do well in GCSE English? She was. So, when she was not in the room, there was no motivation.

There was an article in the *Times Educational Supplement* on the work that I do with students on motivation and goal-setting which referred to me as a 'Mr Motivator'. My role, however, is not to go out and motivate people. I am too busy motivating myself to get out of bed at 5.00 a.m. What I want to share with young people – and less youthful people who will listen – are the strategies and techniques for motivating themselves and, as far as I am concerned, having a big enough 'why' has got to be number one on the list.

Japanese culture has a form of internal motivation known as 'mastery'. This is the process of trying to be better than no one other than yourself. You are engaging in an activity to be the best you can be in that activity. Working through the belts in various martial arts works in this way. You are allowed to progress only when you have mastered everything involved in your current level. Indeed, the after-school maths club Kumon works along similar principles – progression through perfection. Yet, for many, the school system moves us forward whether we have taken on board the basics or not – progression through propulsion.

Motivation through trying to be better than ourselves is a process that the seminal achievement researcher Mihaly Csikszentmihalyi refers to as 'ipsative assessment'. Am I better than I was yesterday? You might know it as the PB approach beloved of all Sportspeople – the Personal Best.

'I do not try to be better than anyone else. I only try to dance better than myself.'

Dancer Mikhail Baryshnikov on ipsative referencing in tights.

One of the most successful coaches in American basketball history was a gentleman called John Wooden, who secured ten national titles in just twelve years and was unbeaten in four of those seasons. When asked the secret of his success he tells the story of how his father, a simple farmer, told him his personal secret for happiness:

> Never try to be better than anyone else … but always try to be the best you can be.

'The gulls who scorn perfection for the sake of travel go nowhere slowly. Those who put aside travel for the sake of perfection go anywhere instantly.'

Elder gull Chiang to Jonathan Livingston Seagull on the need to be our best. And he is a seagull, so it must be true.

This is the real essence of the spirit of internal motivation, and it flies in the face of the pressures that schools have been under most recently through league tables, and that learners have been under traditionally through the top-of-the-class versus bottom-of-the-class process.

What a top basketball coach can teach us about education

In his book *Practical Modern Basketball*, John Wooden says: 'True success can be attained only through self-satisfaction in knowing that you did everything within the limits of your ability to become the very best you are capable of becoming.'

Yes, we all have limits, yet we are all capable of achieving success. So few schools I have been in, especially at secondary level, really go out of their way to reinforce the genuine successes of all their students, not just the laureates – sporting or academic. If your success is measured by looking at those around you and having more, faster, achieving better or any variation on a similar theme, then you will be forever doomed to a sense of failure and despondency. There will always be those around you who are bigger, better, prettier, faster or whatever. Yet, as soon as you stop looking over your shoulder and focus on your own continuous improvement, things really begin to happen. The two most important questions to ask are, first, am I doing my best and, second, am I better than I was last time? Or, as Wooden continues:

> 'Therefore, in the final analysis, only the individual himself can correctly determine his success.'

To what extent in school do we encourage the first question, bearing in mind the system of marks, tests and exams? ('I'm good at geography because the teacher says I am.' 'I've done an essay but I won't know how good it is until the teacher has marked it.') Even the mark for effort that some schools pursue is still usually the teacher's interpretation of how hard the student has tried and, while this may be a half-decent indicator at times, it is still an external viewpoint and susceptible to bias ('She's a nice girl and always tries hard') or manipulation ('You've applied yourself really well to this project, you've been hunched over that computer for hours … ').

There is another downside to praise at work here too – if we overpraise then the child might do just enough to receive the praise and then stop. When do we praise? When the child has reached our level of expectation.

One primary school I worked with has a sticker system for when a child hands in a piece of work; green means 'I tried very hard', orange means 'I tried fairly hard' and red means 'I didn't try at all'. This is then used as a starting point for a conversation with the child about effort and motivation. Not only does this emphasise the whole notion of effort by making it explicit, it also helps children learn that success and achievement need to come from within, that external praise and recognition are nice but not essential for success.

> 'I do not recognise anyone's right to one minute of my life. Not to any part of my energy. Not to any achievement of mine.'
>
> Fictitious architect Howard Roark (based on real-life architectural innovator Frank Lloyd Wright) in *The Fountainhead* by Ayn Rand.

So, can I look at myself in the mirror at the end of the day and say, 'Today, I did all I could to be all I could'? Remember, that is as much a question for you, the teacher and role model, as it is for the child. And, second, 'Am I better today that I was yesterday?', because only then will I know if I am making progress, regardless of the achievements of others. John Wooden describes the hopelessness of basing happiness and success on comparison with others:

> There is nothing wrong in striving for an 'A' mark and wanting to win a contest, but we must face the fact that we are not all created equally as far as mental and physical ability is concerned, we are not all raised in the same environment, we will not all have the same foundation in English or in athletics and we will not all have the same facilities with which to work. However, if success and satisfaction can only be achieved by

making a superior mark in a class or by winning a contest, many students are going to be dissatisfied.

In the face of external pressures (SATs, GCSEs, league tables, inspections – for a start) I know it is hard for teachers to push against the system and focus on such advice, yet perhaps that is what makes it even more vital that teachers use their tremendous power to achieve it. In doing so a future generation will learn to live by their own standards and not live a life of desperate and doomed one-upmanship and underachievement.

Yet competition is not all bad. The competitive element to external motivation – sometimes referred to as 'performance' motivation – has a part to play too. This is the motivation to display our talents to others and it incorporates the notion of pitching ourselves against others, one that ties in very neatly with research about the male-type learning brain.

'Girls like non-competitive learning but boys suffer from it.'

The above line is from the fascinating book *Why Men Don't Iron* by Anne and Bill Moir, which illustrates one of many insights into the need for 'differentiation by gender' in our classrooms. Perhaps their most telling insight is as follows:

Equality is confused with sameness and the confusion does neither sex any good ... Males and females are drawn by the biases of their brains to learn in different ways and to have different interests and enthusiasms and any educational system that insists that boys and girls are the same, and must therefore be treated the same, is set to do damage.

What does this mean for motivation in your classroom? For a start, make sure you have female-type learning opportunities – cooperative, collaborative, language-based – as well as male-type learning – competitive, physical, emotional, with an emphasis on symbols and things.

Although top sportspeople consistently talk about the need to focus on their PB and highlight the fact that during a race they are not constantly looking over their shoulders to see where the competition is, part of their training does involve assessing where they are in relation to that competition. What do they need to do to be up there with the best? It is a combination of mastery and performance that seems to work better than either concept standing alone. And both work better alone than a third form of motivation that can be referred to quite simply as 'fear'.

We all know that fear is a motivator. We all have stories of a teacher – it is often a History teacher – who forced us to achieve History O-level through brute force and blind fear. Did we enjoy the lessons? No, we dreaded them. Do we have an abiding love for history? Probably not, more likely a serious history phobia. After all, being bitten by a dog motivates you to run from, and not towards, other dogs.

Motivation for athletes

Sportspeople tend to have two sorts of motivation:
1   motivation to win (forget how you played);
2   motivation to play well (forget whether you won).

According to sports psychologist Dr Stuart Biddle from the University of Exeter, the ideal is 'to win, to win well and to be motivated by improvement'. Males, he notes, seem to lean towards the former, females to the latter. Parents have an influence here too. When the child comes through the door after the match do they ask, 'Did you win?' (motivation type 1) or 'Did you play well?' (motivation type 2)?

The message for us, as teachers, is to encourage a passion for a subject and a passion for excellence with high expectations all round, combined with a healthy amount of competitive spirit and public performance.

One of the differences between external and internal motivation can be found in the difference between rewards and celebrations. In the former, we bribe an individual to do something they did not necessarily want to do – 'If you do this then you will get that'. In the latter, we celebrate with them what they were doing anyway. Consider it from your own point of view – there is a big difference between the headteacher of a school saying, 'If we have a good term I'll bring in a bottle of wine on the last day' and one morning finding a tin of biscuits in the staff room with a little note saying how well you are doing so far this term and to keep up the good work.

In other words

- Help identify the purpose and relevance of what you are teaching.
- Teach and model goal–setting strategies.
- Help children set their own individual targets.
- Encourage and adopt high, positive expectations and standards.
- Be aware of the challenges of the world beyond school.
- Let them fail in a positive way.
- Celebrate rather than reward.

Chapter 2

Go with the flow

Want to know the secret of happiness? Then check out the work of the man with the impressive name that I quoted in the previous chapter, Mihaly Csikszentmihalyi. He has written one of the most influential books in the area of personal development in the last hundred years, the ultimate guide, if you like, to being happy. It is called *Flow*, and subtitled *The Psychology of Happiness*.

Csikszentmihalyi and his students travelled the world to talk to individuals from different cultures with various lifestyles and livelihoods to find out what it is that makes us happy. What he discovered is that happiness has nothing to do with external factors but is to do with achieving a particular state of mind. But before I reveal what that is, let's take a closer look at that word 'state'. Of all the keys to effective learning that research throws up, it is the 'state' that we are in when we learn which comes through time and time again as the single most important factor in the learning process.

> 'You can't play the violin if you have just been using a large hammer.'
>
> Einstein on why the lesson your students have just come from can make or break your own lesson.

'State' includes, for example, what the look on our faces is like and what our breathing is doing. It is the muscular tension in our bodies, the chemicals and emotions in our brains and bodies. If we are in the wrong state for learning, then we will be unable to learn as effectively as we could otherwise. Indeed, who knows what damage is being done to our long-term perception of learning by being taught in a way that has no regard for our learning state. Remember the teacher who had you sitting at your desk for the entire double period on a Friday afternoon, heads down, working in complete silence?

How not to light up the classroom

Writing in the *Sunday Times* on the negative effects of fluorescent lights in the classroom, Dr Fritz Hollowich said:

> These findings explain the agitated mental and physical behaviour of children staying the whole day in school under artificial illumination which has strong spectral deviation from sunlight.

Apart from not containing the full spectrum of light that our brains need, they also flash on and off around 100 times a second, inducing in us 'stress type' levels of the hormones cortisol and ACTH. (And, according to Dr John Newcomber at the Washington University of Medicine, cortisol 'interferes with the energy supply to brain cells used to recall facts'.) In a relaxed state the brain is processing information at about five to ten times per second, which can be multiplied by twenty during prolonged exposure to fluorescent lights. And we wonder why children are stressed, intellectually tired, restless and agitated?

Learning in a negative state will not only close us down but can also lead us to associate learning with negative feelings for the rest of our lives. My father was taught to read Shakespeare in time to a metronome and for many years had trouble even driving through Stratford-upon-Avon. (The advent of the Stratford bypass has helped him travel to Evesham, but he still grows pale at the merest whiff of iambic pentameter.) However, by focusing overtly on creating a positive state for learning in our lessons, we start to make associations in the students' brains between learning and pleasure that will last them a lifetime.

Enthusiasm

Enthusiasm is a fantastic word. It comes from the Greek *enthousiazein* meaning 'the god within'.

> **'People who are successful usually have an inner drive about them.'**
>
> **Alex Ferguson taking a peek inside a Manchester United shirt.**

Good teachers know that enthusiasm is contagious. What we sometimes forget is that lack of enthusiasm is also contagious. We can bring children up or drag them down by the way that we are when we address them in assembly, when we stand before them in the classroom, when we pass them in corridors, when we push in front of them in the dinner queue. Remember that the next time you are standing up to give an assembly or a staffroom briefing. I have seen so many young people come away from an assembly with their enthusiasm for the day sucked out of them before they have even started – not to mention the staff in a similar state after the morning briefing. In which other industry would you start the day with a demotivational team talk?

> 'What you are shouts so loudly in my ears that I can't hear what you say.'
>
> Ralph Waldo Emerson, reminding us that male teachers should choose their ties with care.

Although some people claim that when we communicate only 7 per cent of that experience is in the words, 55 per cent is body language and 38 per cent is down to the tone of voice, this is not genuinely the case. There is much more to it than that. That said, how we say what we say can make a great deal of difference. I once heard a 'train manager' break the news of a 15-minute delay in such a way that a carriage full of tired commuters simply responded by laughing.

> 'In the right key one can say anything. In the wrong key, nothing: the only delicate part is the establishment of the key.'
>
> George Bernard Shaw on how much you can get away with if you have a smile on your face.

What, then, are the real messages we are passing to young people if we are not careful? According to Dr Emanuel Donchin at the University of Illinois, 99 per cent of what children learn at school is not what we think we are teaching them but what they pick up through the way we dress, the way we look, the way we say things, the environment, the hidden agendas, the relationships we have. When we heave a sigh and tell students in a resigned and negative manner, 'We've got a training day tomorrow', we are doing more than saying tomorrow will be a training day. We are sending a powerful message about how reluctant we are to learn anything new. We may as well be saying, 'Learning! Who wants to bother with that? Get on with your work, you!'

Your enthusiasm for your subject, for your job, for young people, for life, will come through. You may be the only person in a child's life who is passionate about anything so it is down to you to teach them – by example – how much can be achieved with passion. Anita Roddick once said that if she had to put her success down to any one thing she would put it down to 'passion'. Think of it as one of the positive emotions that help us to access the brain's limbic system to open up the 'learning brain' (of which more later). Without it we are never going to tap into what the students have to offer. Help them understand that skill alone is not enough to excel in life. Passion will take them further.

> 'Great dancers are not great because of their technique: they are great because of their passion.'
>
> The late, great dancer Martha Graham on how to achieve the 'great' bit.

I have just come back from a half-day's INSET event with a group of teachers at a school in the north of England. The issue they had, which had been picked up at their recent inspection, was that the students were not independent in their learning and lacked motivation. The teachers were pleasant enough, but some turned up late, most sat at the back and one came up to me to ask if it was worthwhile them having pen and paper and if they would have to make notes. What would be said to a student who turned up in such a manner for a lesson and then asked the teacher whether there was anything worth learning going on in this lesson?

If young people are so susceptible to the messages we give out it is important that we 'walk the talk'. In the words of Mahatma Gandhi: 'Be the change you want to see in the world'.

The ideal learning state, according to Csikszentmihalyi, is one that combines high levels of challenge with low levels of stress, something he refers to as 'flow'. Think of it as illustrated in Figure 2.1. Start in the bottom left square – imagine, as a confident driver, you are trying to perform a hill start in your car but being watched by a policeman who suspects you have been drinking. And you have your in-laws in the back seat. Alternatively, just think – Ofsted inspection. The bottom right square could be wordsearch territory. Moving to the top left square – you remember your very first day as a newly qualified teacher, don't you? And the top right square is where the flow lives!

Another name for flow is, to use a phrase from the world of sport, to be 'in the zone'. Top-class sports people know that to perform at their peak level the 'zone' is where they have to be – in other words, in their optimum performance state. They have to have a challenge worthy of their adrenal glands but do their best to minimise – but not eradicate completely – the levels of stress they are experiencing. A version of this 'in the zone'

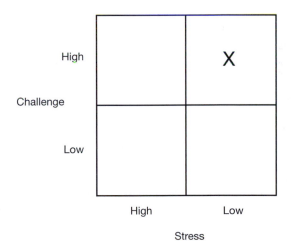

Figure 2.1 The ideal learning state (adapted from Csikszentmihalyi 1992).

phenomenon is often experienced by people on computers. Have you ever promised your better half you'll be just ten minutes on your laptop or playing Solitaire on your phone, or indeed writing a book, only to surface three hours later to find your dinner in the dog? The best evidence of this in the classroom comes from those occasions when, at the end of the period, you have to remind the children that the lesson has finished and that it is time to move on, or when they say words to the effect of 'I like doing that, it's not like learning … '.

This 'flow' state consists, then, of the two important sub-states: high challenge and low stress. Note, especially, that we are not saying 'no stress' but 'low stress'. Stress has had a great deal of bad press in recent years; it has been blamed for all sorts of things from ongoing minor coughs and colds to serious mental illness and cancer. The ability of our thoughts and beliefs to affect our health is called psycho-neuroimmunology, and is described in the fascinating book *The Sickening Mind* by Paul Martin. Apparently, during the Gulf War, more people were killed in Israel by the *stress of the threat* of Scud-missile attacks than by actual strikes by the Iraqis. Yet stress is a natural response, and necessary for us to function effectively. A stress-free life is no life at all. It is our *response* to stress that decides what happens to us – not the stress itself. Or, put another way, it is the responsibility – *response-ability* – we take when it comes to dealing with the natural and necessary stresses of daily life that make the real difference. Two people are made redundant: one person goes to pieces, the other person flourishes with his or her new-found freedom and control. It is not what happens outside of us that makes the difference, it is what happens inside of us as a result of what happens outside of us.

While we are on the subject, how are you modelling the role of taking responsibility? For every ten schools I come across in which staff moan that they used to be able to do this or that until the National Curriculum or Ofsted came along, I will meet one where they are simply getting on and making things work anyway. In Scotland, teachers I met talked about 'guidelines, not tramlines'. Tom Peters, the American business guru, once said, 'Empowerment is a state of mind'. It's true. When I asked the head of one primary school about the literacy hour, she simply replied, 'Oh, we don't do that!'; not 'we don't do that because it's not important', but 'as accountable and responsible professionals, we will do what we know to be best for our children'. When I asked her about the legal obligation to do it she replied, 'Well, who checks?' Another primary headteacher I met recently told me that they 'don't do Fridays any more'. In other words, once a week they drop the statutory curriculum and do what they feel – know – to be right to add value to the children's lives in their school. 'And when the inspector comes to call?' I asked her. 'Tough!' came the reply. Sitting next to her was another primary head who stated that they do the literacy hour four times a week instead of five – the 'rescued' hour they have redeployed for teaching thinking skills. Or, if you want it from an ex-horse's mouth, this is a direct quote from former Chief Inspector of Schools, Chris Woodhead, in reply to a headteacher asking what he was to do with Ofsted recommendations with which he did not concur:

If you don't agree with them you should ignore them.

In other words, if you can justify your position professionally and argue, with evidence, that you know best, then you know best.

'Men must follow the dictates of their conscience, irrespective of the consequences which might overtake them for it.'

Nelson Mandela with a challenge for your conscience.

'Education is too important to be left to teachers' is one quote allegedly from mandarins at Sanctuary Buildings. Another is the idea of introducing a 'teacher-proof curriculum', as there are 'not enough good teachers' to introduce effective reforms. So long as such views prevail, no one will *give* you back your autonomy. What the schools in the above examples have done is simply to take it back for themselves. As Roseanne Barr once said, 'The thing women must learn is that nobody gives you power, you just take it.'

Back in the classroom, 'no stress' means 'forget it': at worst, boredom, leading to frustration and some creative displacement activities – paper aeroplanes, student locked in the cupboard, hitting the fire alarm – or, at best, quietly, dejectedly, passively doing a wordsearch in an out-of-body-experience sort of way in which the hands are doing the exercise but the soul is making paper aeroplanes, locking a student in the cupboard or hitting the fire alarm. Too much stress, on the other hand, can lead to the same results but by a different route. One option when faced with a stressful situation is to opt out altogether. When you are a child of four, you simply lie on the floor kicking your legs and screaming. (Or in the middle of that inspection – you know you want to.) As you get older, other displacement activities kick in (see above, same list).

What stress – or the inappropriate presentation of and approach to dealing with high levels of challenge – does is lead us to engage areas of the brain that have little to do with learning calculus or the conjugation of French verbs, and everything to do with survival, that underlying core focus of our brains. Skip ahead to Chapter 6 for a more detailed look at what is known – metaphorically rather than accurately – as the triune brain model, put forward in 1949 by Dr Paul Maclean. In the meantime, simply be aware that when we are under too much stress we go 'reptilian' – meaning that a basic part of our brains, known as the reptilian brain, or brainstem, and which has little to do with learning and a great deal to do with simply getting by, is being activated. 'High-challenge, low-stress' scenarios ensure that we move beyond this reptilian stage and access the higher, more intellectual areas of our brain.

Another very powerful way of helping students access their flow state in your classroom is through a deeper understanding of what is known as multiple intelligence theory. Just before Christmas a few years ago *The Times* published an article for which the headline read:

Q: What does David Beckham have in common with Albert Einstein?

Underneath was a picture of the great genius who changed the world, despite his odd habits, next to a picture of Albert Einstein. The answer?

A: He is just as intelligent.

Now, for *The Times* to compare David Beckham with Albert Einstein favourably, something has to be afoot – and not before time. At the dawn of the twenty-first century many people feel that it is time to become a whole lot more intelligent about intelligence. And there is no better place to start than with the cornerstone of our definition of intelligence – the intelligence quotient, or IQ.

In his book *The Making of Intelligence*, Ken Richardson, a former lecturer at the Centre for Human Development and Learning at the Open University, wrote this line:

> IQ tests – which fail to clarify what we are measuring, add little to what the teacher can already tell us about pupils in school and have virtually no connection with complex cognitions in the outside world – should be banned.

How many people have had their life blighted – written off even – by the idea of not being very intelligent but being 'good with their hands'? How much genius and richness of human potential and creativity has been denied us by a system that has so narrow a view of intelligence? Indeed, Monsieur Binet, from whose original work the modern-day Stanford–Binet IQ Score grew, would be turning in his grave in Paris if he knew what had been done with his little device, conceived originally to identify – *and then develop* – the potential of children.

'You're not as stupid as our best testing indicates.'

The Simpsons headteacher Mr Burns on realising that there may be more to Homer Simpson than his IQ score.

Over the past 100 years the IQ score has been sexist (originally boys scored higher than girls, so in 1937 they tweaked it to balance things out), elitist and racist (at the turn of the century, of the 'huddled masses' trying to emigrate to the USA, 87 per cent of Russians, 83 per cent of Hungarians and 79 per cent of Italians were officially 'feebleminded').

'It's not IQ.'

The world's most successful investor, Warren Buffet, on what is not the secret of his success.

I asked a paediatric neurologist recently for his view on IQ, and his reply was that it did have a narrow role as part of a 'battery of tests' in understanding the intellectual power and potential of young people, but that was it. As Gardner himself says in his book *Multiple Intelligences – The Theory in Practice*, 'IQ tests predict school performance with considerable accuracy, but they are only an indifferent predictor of performance in a profession after schooling'. I would suggest that even their success in a school environment is more a reflection of what that school is focusing on than on any magic in the IQ test itself.

Two of the biggest flaws regarding an IQ-based view of human potential are:

1   Our intelligence is fixed;
2   Our intelligence is a single factor, something you either have or don't have to varying degrees.

To refute the first one, simply look at the work being done throughout the world in the area of raising people's intelligence through effective thinking skills. Even Monsieur Binet himself was able to teach memory strategies to some of his most intellectually challenged students, which enabled them to succeed at a memory test that had the school inspectors stumped.

'If the human brain were simple enough to understand, we'd be too simple to understand it.'

Victor Lewis-Smith on why, despite the 1990s being the 'Decade of the Brain' and a time of great discovery in our understanding of what is going on between our ears, we still know very little.

To understand the idea that we can 'grow' our brains, consider the process of learning from a neurological point of view. In many ways, learning is the growing of connections between brain cells. Put simply, learning is about making and then strengthening tentacle-like connections that link up the hundreds of billions of brain cells to send electrical energy jumping about across neural networks. What this means, however, is that the more connections we make *the more connections we can make*. Think of telephone lines. If you had had a telephone fifty years ago, how many people could you have rung? Compare that number with the number of people you could call today. The more connected a system, the more connected it can become. What's more, we actually change the structure of our brains by what we do with them daily. (This is similar to the way in which our bones adapt to use; for example, the bones in the forearms of tennis players adapt over time to suit their sport.)

$$\frac{n(n-1)}{2} = x$$

This is Metcalfe's Law: the usefulness, or utility, of a network equals the square of the number of users – where n is the number of points in a network and x is the number of possible connections available to that network. In relation to your brain, for n read one hundred billion, and let your imagination do the rest.

So we really do, literally, 'grow our brains': the more we use them, the more we can use them; the more we learn, the more we can learn. To improve our intelligence and creativity we should seek to grow the number of connections we make, to maximise what Nobel laureate, economist and psychologist Herb Simon refers to as 'the network of possible meanderings'. A great deal of research has been done on what the scientists call 'environmental enrichment', that is to say stimulating brain development and health through the challenge and complexity it is exposed to. Recent research is finding that we not only enrich our brains this way but also prevent and mitigate a range of brain disorders including, according to The Dana Foundation, 'major neurodegenerative diseases (Alzheimer's, Parkinson's and Huntington's); neurological injuries like stroke, head injury and epilepsy, and addictive disorders including fetal alcohol syndrome and cocaine or amphetamine addiction.'

My advice to young people is to regularly do a 'work out' on their brains. Once a week read a page of a newspaper they would not normally read, watch a documentary they would not normally watch, and to eat something different, smell something different, touch something new once a fortnight. One of the most intelligent and creative people I have ever met is a man now working for a highly innovative software company who told me that he didn't do very well at school, but when he was little his mother used to sit him in front of Open University on television at 6.00 a.m. so that she could have a lie-in. He was convinced that this exposure to new ideas had had an impact on the way his mind worked in adulthood. Houdini used to refer his students to the idea of 'polymathic proficiency' – knowing a lot about a lot. Darwin's ideas fermented in his head after the reading of anything from *Cottage Gardener and Country Gentleman's Companion* to the *Indian Sporting Review* and the *Philosophical Transactions of the Royal Society of London*, according to David Jones in his book *Almost Like a Whale*, in which he cites Darwin's claim that his mind was 'a machine for grinding general laws out of a large collection of facts'.

There is a whole arsenal of thinking skills programmes currently available to educators to help young people 'grow their intelligence'. These include Instrumental Enrichment, its distant cousin the Somerset Thinking Skills Course, Philosophy for Children and the series of Cognitive Acceleration programmes that started with Science (Cognitive Acceleration in Science Education – CASE) and now includes Geography (CAGE), maths (CAME), Technology (CATE), Religious Education (CARE) and French (CAFE – actually I lied about that, I just think there should be one for French). There is also a more generic set of materials for key stage 1 now, entitled, with almost religious determination, Let's Think, useful for at least one daily act of joint cognition.

Instrumental enrichment

In the new Israel in the 1950s a psychologist called Reuven Feuerstein was working with young people with severe emotional, behavioural and learning difficulties, who had come to the Middle East via the concentration camps and from the displaced Jewish communities of North Africa. Feuerstein was working on the premise that these children had missed out on the role that the adult plays in 'mediating' between the outside world and the developing connections in the child's brain.

For example, babies can see at an earlier age than was once thought, but the process is one of scanning rather than focusing. An adult in a loving – or at least attentive – relationship with a child actually teaches that child how to focus. Focused concentration is a learned skill, passed from adult to child, like talking or walking. (One of the forerunners of today's thought-controlled computer games was a helmet designed to help children learn how to focus their concentration by linking their brain patterns to a dot on the screen that they moved by their thoughts.) However, if you put into a classroom a child who can naturally scan but has not yet learned focusing, what will be the result? It is little surprise that the child can end up, quite literally, all over the place – both physically and mentally. And then we complain that the child is 'unteachable'.

Instrumental Enrichment comprises many things, including a series of 'instruments' – intellectually challenging exercises to 'wire up' the child's brain so that it can focus – and its use often has dramatic results.

The second flaw with the narrow IQ-based view of intelligence is brought into focus by the work of Howard Gardner at Harvard University and takes us back to that article in *The Times*. Although it claimed that Einstein and Beckham were equally intelligent, it was not being suggested that they were *intelligent equally*. Rather, they were high-profile embodiments of *two different forms* of intelligence, namely 'logical/mathematical' for Einstein and 'body/physical' for Beckham. One of the early questions that puzzled Gardner was the idea that if you took a Wall Street trader and a native aboriginal Australian, both highly intelligent in their own world, and swapped them over, where would their intelligence go? Who would last longer?

This multiple intelligence (MI) theory started off with seven different intelligences; is now up to eight, and could be joined by more, as it is a work in progress. There could – even should – be many more. Let me take you through the list in the way that I do during my INSET sessions.

There is a process from learning science called 'pre-exposure'. By giving students a taster, a trailer to what they will be doing soon, we are able to speed up the learning process. To understand this better, think of learning as the game of 'Skatch' in which a tennis ball is thrown to be caught by someone wearing a Velcro glove to which it sticks – catch for people who can't catch. Think of the tennis ball as the new knowledge and the glove as our existing knowledge. We learn best by hooking new knowledge onto things for which we already have connections. This is one of the reasons why metaphors and similes work so well. If I am told, 'He's as brave as a lion', then I can quickly take on board the sort of person he is, as this new fact hooks into my existing knowledge about lions. Or, if you say an acre is 4,840 square yards, I look blankly at you, but if you say, 'That's about the size of a football pitch', I can immediately comprehend the size.

With that in mind, let me take you through the eight intelligences in a way that I know makes them far easier to understand and remember and speeds up the whole learning process, compared with simply using their official – and abstract – names. As you read these names (and feel free to update or adapt them to your own time and culture) try and work out which is the intelligence area most closely linked to these people; think of which one is most closely aligned with your own strengths and also think about children you are working with who perhaps are not doing brilliantly in your lessons. Where does their genius lie? Or, to rephrase an old question, ask not 'how clever are you?' but 'how are you clever?'

- Einstein
- Princess Diana
- Mother Teresa
- Picasso
- The AA man
- Mozart
- Charlie Dimmock
- Shakespeare.

This is the sort of list of corresponding intelligences you should have.

- logical/mathematical
- interpersonal
- intrapersonal

- visual/spatial
- body/physical
- musical
- naturalistic
- verbal/linguistic

Now, surely this model of intelligence gives us a bit more room to play with in the classroom. Rather than dismissing children with high body/physical abilities but lower logical/mathematical abilities as simply 'good with their hands', we can start to make them feel as good about themselves and what they have to offer society as our more traditional high-flying Oxbridge types. If nothing else, in Gardner's words, 'Multiple Intelligences can be a useful inventory'.

Imagine your classroom and, as you look around the learners in front of you, you notice that the eight people above are actually in your class. What tasks would you set them to allow them to play to their strengths at least once over the course of the lesson?

What now follows are some ideas to get you started.

Logical/mathematical

Puzzles, charts, graphs, analysis, conclusions, forecasts, predictions, sequences, consequences, statistical work, ratios (for example of adverbs to adjectives in a particular poem and for what effect), inducing general rules (for example, drawing grammatical rules from sequences of a foreign language or spotting the spelling rule 'i before e except after c').

I once worked with a group of year 9 students in the middle of London using multiple intelligences as a model for helping them with their SATs. The school had split the year into three, stratifying them by ability (academic, of course), and it was the afternoon by the time I had the 'less able' students in front of me in the library (or learning resources centre, as we now have to call them). These were the sort of students that I knew the school, like many others, had written off as the difficult and/or thick kids, whose only aspirations could be to work in the factories or the supermarkets (or comestible replenishment centres). My genial host for the day was a deputy who introduced me to the students thus:

> Right you lot, settle down. Now some of you are lazy. Some of you are stupid. This is Mr Gilbert here to work with you. You listen to him and it might just make a difference!

I recount this story when I deliver my INSET work and it usually receives somewhere between a laugh and a gasp. Yet, how often are such events being repeated up and down the country, either explicitly, as on this occasion, or sometimes more surreptitiously? I am told that one professor of education shares the story of being shown around a school by a proud headteacher until they came across a marvellous piece of sculpture in the foyer which the professor commented upon admiringly. 'Yes, it is good,' said the headteacher, 'and it's by one of our less able kids too.' (As one teacher pointed out to me recently, do we ever have less able children in our schools who are good at Maths?)

Another time I was working with a group of 'underachieving' students in a top school in Wales. Because of the novel nature of the work we were doing and the fact that the school had an eye for PR, the local press had been asked to come in to capture the moment. The photographer who arrived looked at me and said something to the effect of, 'You're here to work with the thick kids today then are you?'

> **'Do you think I would have amounted to anything if I went to school? University-trained scientists only saw that which they were taught to look for and missed the great secrets of nature.'**
>
> **Inventor Thomas Edison on what he learned from not being taught.**

Now, academically, it is unlikely that these students would set the world alight (although not impossible). If Einstein had been at that school, he would probably have been in that group – not to mention Winston Churchill. And in the eyes of that photographer those children would never aspire to much (perhaps the sort of job that involves looking through a little box with a hole in it and pressing a button), yet young people like that deserve, at a moral, ethical and professional level, *not* to be written off simply because they do not fall within the very narrow academic viewfinder we use to spot potential and ability in schools.

> 'When it comes to the skills that doctors really need – empathy, communications skills, sensitivity, wisdom and maturity – A-levels results tell us little or nothing.'
>
> GP Fred Kavalier writing in 1998 and questioning whether we would ask to see a doctor's A-level certificates before the operation. Elsewhere, I have heard of a personnel manager who used exam results as a way of picking candidates for interview but 'could just as easily have used shoe size or hair colour.

Apart from the many very intelligent people, from Einstein down, for whom school was not an enjoyable experience, there are also so many opportunities to lead a full and happy life without needing to be academic anyway, and for which success at school may actually get in the way. Indeed, as Ken Richardson points out, 'many studies have shown that there is little relation between academic potential and performance in the workplace at any level, even ironically enough, for future academics!' If this is the case, what are we really preparing these high-flying school success stories for? Teaching?

> 'What I discovered was that a Master's in business can sometimes block an ability to master experience.'
>
> Sports promoter Mark McCormack describing 'What they don't teach you at Harvard Business School'. A careers teacher told me once how a personnel manager from a top UK company had described how the hardest part of

her job was telling applicants that, even though they had A grades in all their qualifications and a top degree from Oxford or Cambridge, they were 'still not good enough' to work for the company – not *because* they had the qualifications but because that was *all* they had!

Anyway, back to my year 9 students and their damning introduction by the caring deputy. Now, as a big build-up, it left something to be desired, but at least it gave me the chance to focus immediately on the whole area of intelligence. Without explaining the reasons behind my request I asked them to nod their heads (this can be easier than the more traditional 'raise your hands' if it is a new group and they are a bit shy or reticent for whatever reason) if they could, for example, play a musical instrument well. Then, 'Now nod if you are the team leader, the one the others follow,' and 'Now nod if you like writing little poems or keep a diary,' and so on. They were all able to nod at least once – some more than once. Admittedly we didn't have many logical/mathematical nods but then the group had been pre-selected, as the deputy had made clear.

'The first thing to forget is any notion that you have to be a qualified engineer to make an impact on engineering.'

James Dyson with reassuring words in the light of the shortage of engineers in the world.

I could then begin to explain how some of them were more intelligent than I was in certain areas, capable of doing things that I could not yet do. Once they could see the fine line between 'not able' and 'notable', we could then start to explore how they could use the strengths they had to learn. And very creative they were too. For example Einstein, they said, would turn *Macbeth* into a series of formulae written on a huge board in chalk. Macbeth would be M, Lady Macbeth would be LM. So M + LM = Dangerous Power! Try this one:

$$M - KD = (KM)$$

(Macbeth minus King Duncan equals King Macbeth – but not for long, so put it in brackets.)

Also, while we are combining English with things logical/ mathematical, did you know that, according to Stephen Pinker, 'Ten is in fact the appropriate geometric mean of the number of word choices available at each point in assembling a grammatical and sensible sentence.'

Bear in mind that we tend to make synonymous 'thinking' and 'being logical'. Yet logical thinking is only one particular style of thinking and there are many far more useful ways of thinking, depending on the circumstances, than 'thinking sensibly' all the time. The philosopher Heidegger asked ominously, 'What great danger then moves upon us?' referring to what he called 'calculative thinking' being 'accepted and practised as the only way of thinking'. The need to uphold the value of more 'meditative thinking' was, he said, 'the issue of the saving of man's essential nature'. After all, as Spike Milligan said, 'Where logic fails nonsense can sometimes help you'.

'You are not thinking. You are just being logical.'

Physicist Neils Bohr – but is Dr Spock the only one to succeed in your classroom?

Interpersonal

Group work (collaborative), teamwork (competitive), interviewing, chat shows, drama, teaching others, group leading, group co-ordinating.

A powerful role for the Princess Diana-type in your classroom is to act as the buffer between the teacher and the class. If we are always the first port of call for students with a problem then we will have run ourselves ragged by the end of the lesson, fire-fighting with every hand that shoots up and every cry of 'Miss, what have you got to do, again?' By responding in this way we are not only promoting learned helplessness in our classes but also sending across a powerful message that says – 'There is no need to listen to me when I am giving instructions to the whole class as I will come around and give you one-to-one instruction in just a little while.'

By tapping into the interpersonal talents in the class you can free yourself up to work with those who really do need your support. Princess Diana can sort the others out. She will be learning because she is teaching, as teaching and learning are closely linked anyway, and one of the best ways of learning anything is to teach it to others. Indeed, until you have done that you can never really know if you have learned something. Or, in the words of Virgil, 'As you teach so shall you learn, as you learn so shall you teach.'

Ever done any diving? Me neither, but apparently you always go down in pairs. You 'buddy-up' so that everyone has someone looking out for them. Why not buddy-up in the classroom? For example: 'I commit to you that I will help you get five A–Cs at GCSE or level 5s in your SATs and stay motivated for learning, and you do the same for me. If I get stuck I'll come to you and vice versa. If we both get stuck then we'll go and see Princess Diana. If she's stuck then, and only then, we'll go and bother the teacher'.

Another strategy, in a similar vein, is to have your class learn, for example, half of a chapter each. Then give them five minutes in pairs next time to teach each other their halves, so together they have the whole. One teacher I was told about in the USA has his students revising in pairs, then just before they sit a test, they toss a coin. Whoever loses the toss sits the test but they both share the mark. Be aware also of the distinction between teams and groups. For group work, think collaborative, female brain, cooperation towards a common target. For teamwork, think male brain, competitive work in which the target is to be first, most, longest, fastest, shortest, or whatever.

Intrapersonal

WIIFM?s, empathy, emotional intelligence, metacognition, target setting, goal setting, daydreaming, 'I wonder if … ' statements, 'I feel that … ' statements, 'How would you feel if you were … ?' questions.

If metacognition is a new word to you, how could you work out what it means? How have you worked out the meaning of other new words in the past? How do you personally remember the meanings of new words and phrases? These questions are metacognitive questions. Put simply, it means thinking about thinking. When you have a child who goes from being stuck to being unstuck, rather than simply saying 'Well done,' say 'Well done, how did you do it?' Encourage them to reflect actively on the processes they went through in order to achieve what they did. You may get replies such as 'I dunno,' or 'I just guessed,' but persevere. 'What were the criteria you used for guessing?' 'Which options did you guess, but ruled out?' 'Where did you start from?'

> 'No great discovery was ever made without a bold guess.'
>
> Sir Isaac Newton; millions saw that apple fall, but only Mr Kipling baked a pie.

Another opportunity is that end-of-module test to assess how well they have done. Rather than simply leaving it at that – a grade, a percentage, a score, an average – explore further and spend some time on *how* they have done as well as they did. This also serves as an opportunity for feedback to you, as the teacher, to encourage you to reflect on and improve your own practice. Ask the class which bits they learned quickest and why? What did you do to help them learn? What did you do that perhaps got in the way of their learning? How do they think you could improve your delivery of this module/topic/area next time you come to teach it?

We so often miss out on this metacognitive reflective loop as we hurry from one topic to the next, yet we know that it can raise achievement in the classroom.

'Teachers need to mediate self-searching questions: "How did I succeed?" and "Why did I fail?" are more important for learning than the actual act of succeeding or learning.'

Howard Sharron and M Coulter in *Changing Children's Minds*, on the role that teachers can play in metacognition in the classroom. Indeed, I have been told that a school in New Zealand actually employs a metacognition teacher to help the students learn when they go, for example, on an art trip or to a museum.

Empathy is another important factor as we exploit strengths in intrapersonal intelligence. Questions such as 'How would you feel if … ?' and 'What would you think if … ?' start to address this. 'How would you feel if you were Lady Macbeth?', 'Give me a number between one and ten', 'Five', 'OK, now write a five-word sentence which was the last thing that Macbeth said to himself before he killed Duncan.' Or, 'In no more than nineteen words write down the very last entry in the diary of Stalin/Hitler/Emmeline Pankhurst.' It can also be extended beyond humans – 'How would you feel if you were a rhino being driven from your home by poachers?' or 'Who killed Bambi and how did Thumper feel when he heard the news?' It can even be extended into the inanimate – 'How would you feel if you were a molecule of CFC gas?', 'How would you feel if you were an iceberg shrinking and breaking up, thanks to global warming?'

Take the rain cycle as another example. Traditionally, this is recorded in a combined effort from our logical and visual intelligences. Think of the poster with the rain cycle pictured in stages: 'stage 1, rain falls on mountain'; 'stage 2, water becomes stream', and so on, until you get to stage 5, or so, which is usually, 'water gets picked up by seagulls and taken back to the mountain'. One primary school I went into, however, had allowed a girl to explore this process through the eyes of the raindrop: no pictures or diagrams, just text with comments such as 'I don't remember my Dad because he was rained away when I was only little … '.

Or, how about writing up the experiment from the point of view of what you were experimenting on? (How does that frog feel?) I once had a group of girls writing up the results of dropping lithium into a pot of water from the point of view of the lithium in the form of a letter home. 'Dear Mum, yesterday I fell into a pot of water and you'll never guess what happened … '

One last word here, brought to you from the point where the circles of inter-and intrapersonal intelligence overlap. In their revolutionary and frightening book *The Unfinished Revolution*, John Abbott and Terry Ryan tell how we are born with a range of natural 'predispositions' hard-wired into our brains in order to help us survive. Language is one; or rather the ability to hear sounds and turn them into a very complex system of rules and syntax at a very young age, is one. (This predisposition was famously referred to by the American linguist and campaigner Noam Chomsky as the language acquisition device, or LAD, and is something that is said to die out naturally around the age of 11. And at what age do we start teaching children languages in this country? Exactly!)

Another of these predispositions is the one that leads us to be sociable, gregarious and empathetic individuals, part of a social group. If those elements are not actively stimulated in the child, they will be replaced by other abilities needed for a more solitary life, notably aggression. Like walking, talking and focused concentration, social skills are taught skills that will not necessarily develop without external stimulus.

> 'No man can reveal to you aught but that which already lies half asleep in the dawning of your knowledge.'
>
> Kahlil Gibran in *The Prophet,* backing up the neurological research that, in the words of researcher Michael Gazzaniga (1994), confirms that 'all we are doing in life is catching up with what our brain already knows.'

How can we do this? Rather than simply saying to the child, 'That was naughty what you did to him/her just then!' say instead, 'That was naughty what you did, how do you think he/she feels?' Look for opportunities to exploit actively children's emotional intelligence in that way, and save the world.

Visual/spatial

Learning maps, posters, Mindmaps™, colour, highlighter pens, symbols, icons, visualisation, instructive display work.

To understand the importance of learning in this way let's look again at some important brain research. It has been shown that we have a better memory for pictures than we do for words, that colour co-ordinating our learning improves our memory, that we have 'limitless' memory for concrete visual images, that more of our brain is dedicated to our visual sense than to the other four, that the brain is attracted to colour. And, that when we memorise things using our favourite colour, it improves our memory. This is conclusive evidence, may I suggest, for making sure that learning is more than just black words on a white page, written in a neat manner.

Simple inventions, such as the highlighter pen, can mean the difference between success and failure, yet so few schools seem to encourage children to use them actively. Highlighting keywords is such a useful exercise that can save much time and energy, yet I see so little of it.

Keywords

Tony Buzan, the man behind the many variations on a book on MindMaps®, suggests that 95 per cent of the words that we write traditionally in 'note taking' are a waste of time. So many exercise books are full of so much wasted effort. And, with many girls and some boys, it may well be neat waste, but it is still waste. By thinking in terms of key points and keywords we can save so much time and effort. It helps us make the distinction between 'note taking' and 'note making'. The former goes in the ear and out the pen and bypasses the brain. What looks like learning can be only so much neat recording. The latter, though, has to go through the brain to come out as notes made. The following questions should be actively encouraged in your classroom. Put them on posters and pin them up:

- What do I already know?
- What are the key points?
- Do I agree? Can I think of any examples for which this may not be the case?
- How can I use this?

Again, my experience is that it seems to be more the girls than the boys who are desperate to hang on to all the neat words in their exercise books and are very wary of letting go of what can be more of an emotional than an intellectual prop. Apart from the highlighting of keywords, another strategy is to stick a Post-it® note on each page of the exercise book and write on it no more than about seven words, give or take a couple (we can only hold in our heads about seven chunks of information at any given time, give or take two). That way, when the students are revising they only cover the keywords, but if they get stuck they also have the safety net of the fuller text to fall back into.

I was in a Science lesson recently and a girl had highlighted certain animals in certain colours. I was intrigued as I knew that the school had been doing some work in this area, so I asked the girl why she had chosen to highlight the words in the various colours. 'Because it looks nice,' she replied. Now, I have nothing against work 'looking nice' but this seemed to me like a wasted opportunity. Taking it to the next level, what colour would you highlight carnivores? Herbivores? What, then, about omnivores? Most people come up with red and green for the first two respectively, but things start falling apart after that, with cries of yellow, blue, even orange! However, if we know that red symbolises meat and green symbolises vegetation and we know that the omnivore eats both, we should have both colours involved, so red and green stripes would do it for me. In doing so we move away from what I call the 'tyranny of syntax' – the notion that learning has to be neat words written in a grammatical sentence. Since when? After all, we have spent millions of years learning without written language.

Actively seeking out opportunities to colour co-ordinate learning in your lessons is going to help tap into your Picasso skills – points *for* an argument in green, points *against* in red; sea-dwelling creatures in blue, land-dwellers in green; masculine words in blue, feminine words in red, neuter words ... you choose.

One of the most widespread, misunderstood and controversial Picasso-esque strategies for learning is the one for which Tony Buzan coined (and then registered) the name MindMaps®. I have given up being explicit in talking about them these days when working with either students or teachers as there are so many people out there with a very negative view of these tools. (Indeed, in and around the Swindon area you can't mention them at all without a collective groan from the audience, thanks, so I gather, to a major event at the town's showground on the subject, led by a Mr Tony Buzan!)

However, what if I were to tell you that I met an English teacher in a school in Birmingham who claimed that a high proportion of her students achieved A★ grades in GCSE English last year by using these Knetworks, many of them inner-city Black boys, for whom such a result is, statistically speaking, surprising? And what if I add that when I asked her what she thought they would have achieved if they hadn't been introduced to this strategy, she replied that it would have been nearer

D grades? Or, how about I tell you of the student I met who had used this technique all the way through his GCSEs, his A–levels, right through to Liverpool University from which he emerged with a 2:1 in Geography, and who had chosen to use it because he was lazy? 'I want to put the least amount of effort in to get the most amount of benefit out,' is how he described to me his criteria for choosing a learning style.

'Losers give it their all.'

Boxing promoter Don King reinforcing the 'least in, most out' key to success; or if you prefer your quotes from a more literary source, how about Bertolt Brecht's, 'Great men sweat too much'?

(This search for languor, by the way, is actually quite natural and not simply the male brain's quest for an easy life. Your heart is not beating too hard while you sit there reading this book – it is expending the least amount of effort necessary to get by. The same applies to your breathing. Exciting as the area of learning and motivation may be, you are not sitting there panting with your heart pounding while you read this particular book.

There have been many books written in this area – most of them by Tony Buzan himself – and I do recommend having a look and having a go. Not only do they hit the spot when it comes to tapping into your visual/spatial intelligence and help certain boys to learn by moving away from having so many words to write or read, they also work in a very whole-brain manner, linking the ways of thinking traditionally associated with the left brain – language, sequences, component parts, logic, concrete reasoning – with those more right-brain (and hugely overlooked) thinking elements – colour, shapes, movement, pictures, abstract reasoning, space and seeing the big picture. This last element itself is worth the price of a Buzan book. How often do we show our learners one tiny piece of the big picture at a time and wonder why they switch off? If I said to you that we were going to do a jigsaw puzzle together, that it would take two years, that you would only be allowed to work on it for an hour or so a week, that I was only going to give you a couple of pieces at a time, and that I wasn't going to let you see what the picture on the cover looked like until the end, how would you feel? I am fairly confident that you would quickly become very disillusioned with my GCSE jigsaw class. Yet, are we doing the same thing in our lessons by not letting them see the big picture from the outset?

This is more than the simple adage of 'telling them what you're going to tell them, telling them, then telling them what you've told them'. It means making sure they know, at any time, where they are going, where they have been and where they are now. Think of it like a street plan. If I were taking you to Paris for the first time you would need a map to answer all those questions, you would need to be able to 'helicopter' above the streets – in your head at least – to help you fight the frustration of only having a part of the bigger picture. Indeed, the only person I've ever met who became excited when asked to direct me to the railway station in Milton Keynes was a man who had once worked for the Milton Keynes Development Agency. He had been above the town in a helicopter and could see how it was mapped out in a logical and easy-to-understand way that is denied to us ground-dwellers (highlighted in brown).

So, apart from the tapping into our visual/spatial intelligence, the effective use of colour co-ordination, the left-brain attributes, the right-brain attributes, the whole-brain activation and the potential for seeing the big picture from the outset, what have Buzan's MindMaps® ever done for us? Have they improved our memory?

Researchers once performed an experiment that involved showing volunteers literally thousands of photos of people's faces one day and then the following day showing them thousands more. On the second day, however, photos from the day before were shown side by side with new, but quite similar, portrait shots. The ability of the students to distinguish those previously seen from similar but new faces was amazing, to the point where the researchers gave up the experiment, concluding that there was effectively 'no limit' to our memory for concrete visual images.

Sitting in an exam, it is far easier to remember the 'picture' of our learning than it is all those abstract words on the page. Our 'lazy' boy said that he felt he was 'cheating' when he sat his finals. Because he had drawn up his model essay answers using these MindMaps®, sitting in an exam it was easy for him to recreate his revision by drawing on his visual memory. So, within a few minutes of starting his exam he was sitting there with his notes in front of him. 'I knew exactly what grade I was going to get before I had even finished the paper,' he said. I have even now heard of staff at one secondary school that erected a huge, blank screen in their exam hall by draping a large, white sheet over the climbing rails on the walls. They then encouraged the students to project the image of their MindMaps® on to this screen during the exam and, in doing so, tapped into the power of MindMaps®, the students' visual/spatial intelligence and the power of the human brain to see things that aren't there, simultaneously. And, if you need any further proof of the need for prioritising our visual/spatial intelligence in the classroom, then, as with so much of our understanding of how to get more out of more people, let's go back to the evolution of the brain.

More of our brain is dedicated to our visual sense than to any of the other four. Much of this visual processing takes place at the back of our brains. Bear this in mind when you realise that, as we move from babyhood to maturity, our brains wire themselves up from the back to the front (the same way that a school hall fills for an INSET session). Our visual abilities develop far faster than the sorts of brain activities associated with the front of the brain, normally abstract and intellectual reasoning. It is more important for a baby to recognise its mother than to consider how fast it would travel through space in a lift.

During our evolution the huge growth spurt in our brains came about when we moved from using all fours to two legs, and dramatically increased our hunting range. The explosion in our visual senses, and the corresponding size of our brains, came about as our hunting ancestors started moving further afield and not only had to remember where the best hunting grounds were but also how to get back home again for tea. This may also explain the differences in the visual processing power of the male and female brains, with, research suggests, the female brain less able to manipulate three-dimensional objects through space in their heads (who shouted 'reverse-parking cars'?) because, in evolutionary terms, they didn't have to. Evolution apparently also explains why the male eye works best for seeing single items at a distance (a blonde at a party, a hand-ball incident in the penalty box) but is unable to spot a new bottle of ketchup in a cupboard.

Our evolution, which means in essence who we are and how we operate, and the world of pictures and images go hand in hand. From cave paintings to hieroglyphics, a picture really is worth a thousand words, and tapping into the visual/spatial intelligence of all your students is crucial to unlocking what they have to offer the world at large, let alone your Science or History class.

Mackenzie Thorpe is one of the most sought-after contemporary artists in the world today. It is one of his pictures that adorns the front cover of this book, and deliberately so. Would you have spotted his gift if he had been in your class? Do you have the next Mackenzie Thorpe sitting in your detention at this very moment or struggling over his next essay assignment? This is his story in his own words.

> I was the oldest of seven children, born into a three-bedroom council house in Middlesborough. My father was a labourer, with no trade qualifications. There was no luxury. Three pennies a week would be pocket money – if I got any. But at that age you don't know you're poor. I thought where I lived was the biggest town in the world, like any other kid does.

I've always drawn. And when I drew, I'd go into my own world. I'd spend my time getting cigarette packets, unwrapping them, flattening them and drawing on them. I'd just draw and draw and draw.

I knew I was going to be a painter. I think I was eleven when I saw *Lust for Life*, the film about Van Gogh. I really identified with Van Gogh, especially in the scene where everyone is shouting at him, making fun of him. That sort of thing happened to me all the time because I didn't fight back. Nobody understood me. And I didn't even know what it was they couldn't understand.

I left school at fifteen. I couldn't get any qualifications because of my dyslexia. I did all sorts of jobs, working on ships up and down the Tees, often on the dole. It was a bad time for me, and I was really unhappy. One day a friend suggested I go along to the art college.

My application form was terrible, the spelling was all wrong and it was clear enough that I couldn't write essays. But I had literally thousands of drawings. At that time I used to carry an old school blackboard around on my back. I fixed a drawing board onto it, and some haversack straps. I was out at six in the morning drawing in the parks, everywhere. And because I had this huge pile of work there was no problem at the college – I was in!

I had no confidence at all when I started there. If somebody had said I was blue I'd have believed them. I put all my gear in a bag with 'Karate' written on the side so people would think I was some kind of martial arts expert and leave me alone!

Seeing the paintings in the Tate Gallery for the first time changed my whole way of thinking. From then on I just ate and drank modern art. Rothko, especially, is one of my real heroes. I realised how important it was to put myself, Mackenzie Thorpe, into my paintings.

I particularly like that last line. How it took him a long time to have the confidence to realise that he, Mackenzie Thorpe, had something to offer the world, that he needn't simply be a copy of others who had come before him – 'second handers' as Ayn Rand calls them in her book *The Fountainhead* – but that he could be, indeed needed to be, a unique individual in his own right in order to succeed. My success at school was largely due to being able to think like others thought – not to think anything new but to think what others already knew. That was why I was rewarded. It was only after leaving the education system that I realised that you can't follow the herd and lead the field at the same time. Are the children leaving your school ready to stand out or simply stand to? Do they leave with the desire to be a someone or just a somebody? You, their teacher, have such a crucial role to play in this. Please remember that.

Body/physical

Role play, making models, movement, acting, practical exercises, embodying the learning, walking through the learning, physical cutting and pasting or physical jigsaws.

One school that I worked with a couple of years ago – a very successful state school in the Midlands which had been criticised by inspectors, interestingly enough, for not having enough 'excitement' in its lessons – decided to take the bull by the horns and seek to make lessons rather more 'dangerous' by incorporating these sorts of strategies across the curriculum. The teachers in the English Department, for example, talked about 'physicalising' the learning and introduced strategies such as having students who knew a lot about a new subject go 'up high', others who knew less go 'down low'. So, at times they would have certain students on their chairs, others under the tables (of course that may describe an ordinary lesson of yours). They also started to introduce strategies such as reading out a word and having the students move to the 'verb wall' or to the 'noun wall', depending on what sort of word they thought it was. And, if you weren't sure, you stood somewhere in between depending on how unsure you were.

It doesn't have to be whole-scale running about to begin with. You may have them stand up and point – wall, wall, ceiling, floor: verbs, nouns, adverbs, adjectives – as you read out a passage or poem. They also had students moving seats with each change of the focus of the lesson, a process that not only addressed the physical imperative but also hit the right buttons when it came to state, breaks, energy levels, concentration and breathing.

How to work less and learn more

Have you ever sat through three minutes' worth of advertising in the middle of your favourite programme and then realised that you don't remember any of the commercials, except maybe the first one and the last one? Or have you sat and read a textbook and remember where you started and finished but remember nothing of what went on in the middle? Whenever I am working with underachieving students and ask them to identify the three biggest *obstacles* (notice the language there) to achieving five A–C grades at GCSE there are always two answers that come up time and time again. One is the fact that they blame other people for their shortcomings ('The teachers are crap', 'The school's rubbish', 'My mates keep messing around' – there's a strategy for dealing with that in Chapter 3). The second is that they say they can't concentrate. There seems to be a perception that if they can't sit and concentrate for three hours, then there must be something wrong with them 'so I won't bother at all'.

No matter how inadequate you feel about having a 'lousy memory', the fact that we don't concentrate for long periods of time is just natural and is not the sign of a bad book, commercial break, teacher or learner. It just is.

> 'Time off task at regular intervals is also one of the most important indicators of learning effectiveness.'
>
> Professor John MacBeath on how sometimes the harder we work, the less we learn.

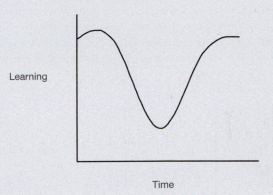

Figure 2.2   The primacy effect and the recency effect.

In the graph showing learning over time (Figure 2.2) you can see how we start well, with learning levels high in the early stages. We even finish on a high. These two features are known, respectively, as the primacy effect and the recency effect. In other words, we remember firsts and lasts but less so middles. (Bear this in mind when you are one of a large number of people being interviewed for a job.) Advertisers are beginning to understand this now, which is why you often see a thirty-second commercial as you start the break and then a ten-second reminder as you come out of the break – a technique called 'a top and a tail'.

In order, then, to stop wasting so much effort, we need to do what the cliché tells us and work smarter, not harder – work less, learn more. If we put a two-minute break in the middle of the period of learning, what is going to happen? Exactly! See Figure 2.3. We should never be working for very long without some sort of break. For exam students, I recommend that they never work for more than about half-an-hour or so without standing up, having a bit of a stretch, doing a bit of exercise. Research has shown that adrenaline released during learning improves our memory – jog on the spot, run up and down stairs, do star jumps. Mind you, it was also found that chocolate has a similar sort of effect – ten press-ups or a Mars bar? You choose!

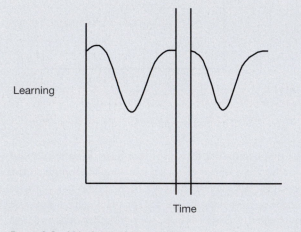

Figure 2.3   Work less, learn more.

Our 'lazy' friend with the MindMaps® recounted how he would prepare for revision by limbering up as if he was about to go and play sport, then blast out a Prodigy or Robbie Williams track, sit down and do half an hour's worth of work, then stand up, walk around, limber himself up again, another blast of music, another half-hour of revision.

> '**I wish I could sit and write for nine hours and then go and watch a film or go for a swim. But instead I write for ten minutes and then break, then write for four minutes, then break. That way nine hours is very quickly filled.'**
>
> **Author Nick Hornby on Classic FM discussing the peak concentration time of the average Arsenal supporter.**

So, the moral is to chunk learning down, break it up, keep an eye on the energy levels, keep an eye on the oxygen levels (just by standing up we increase the amount of oxygen going to the brain by around 15 per cent within less than a minute, which is a crucial factor when you realise that the brain weighs less than 2 per cent of our body weight but takes on board 20 per cent of the oxygen the body consumes) and do just enough often enough to keep going. Or learn to do things, in the words of Don Bennett, the first amputee to reach the 14,410-foot summit of Mount Rainier in the US on one leg and two crutches, when he was asked how he did it, 'one hop at a time'.

The History department in the excitement-seeking school (the one with the Danger and Excitement Group as they referred to the learning project group established to address the issues raised by their inspection) had the tables turned upside-down on top of each other and had the students walking the trenches of the First World War (trenches made of chewing gum). The PE department even had sixth-formers in the hall dressed in coats, gloves, sunglasses and stereo headphones playing badminton, as an exercise in sensory deprivation. (If you teach French, you will know it as the language lab.)

A former colleague of mine was teaching the solar system to a bottom-set group from quite a difficult boys' school. He took them out of the classroom and into the hall, teamed up with the dance teacher and had the group dancing out the learning to Holst's *The Planets Suite* (all but Pluto). In their modular tests the bottom set outperformed the top set. And teachers in a primary school in the north of the country have transformed their lessons by 'physical-ising' their learning with anything from having children jumping from 'column to column', as they act out dividing or multiplying by tens, to starting each morning with a smile and a salsa. The staff are convinced of the benefits of incorporating a physical element to their lessons to improve learning, attitude, motivation, concentration and energy levels – and not just in the children!

Musical

Rhymes, rhythms, raps, ditties, jingles, songs, beats, background music, music that echoes the learning messages, nursery rhymes with new words, football chants.

'Hickory , dickory, dock, the mouse ran up the … .'

You can't help but complete that sentence with the appropriate word even though it may be years since you last heard that particular rhyme. Yet it is the very fact that it does rhyme that helped to make it so easy to learn in the first place and ensures that it sticks. Music – incorporating rhyme, rhythm, dance, emotions, mood, tempo – and memory are powerful allies. Just ask any advertiser. Want people to remember something? Link it in a musical way. Who can use Shake 'n' Vac without humming the tune? Who fails to remember what 'beanz meanz' to a million housewives every day? Then the advertisers went one step further and started using music which had nothing to do with the products themselves to help us remember the ads: from classical – if you're of a certain age, try listening to Bach's *Air on a G String* without hearing a match strike and seeing a plume of cigar smoke wafting up into the air – to pop: think Michael Jackson and Pepsi – to classic pop: again, if you are of a certain age, can you listen to *Heard It On the Grapevine* without taking your trousers off? I know I can't.

Music is such a powerful ally in the classroom:

- it helps get the learners in the right mental state for learning;
- it helps get the teacher in the right mental state for teaching;
- it acts as an anchor – a direct link to feelings and emotions that you can tap into just by playing the theme from *Star Wars* or *Raiders of the Lost Ark*;
- it has been shown to be effective in accelerated learning, especially largos of the Baroque period;
- it can bring learners 'back down' if they come into your lessons over-animated, say from break or directly from a good drama lesson;
- it can bring learners 'back up' if they come in a bit too under-animated, on Monday morning or directly from a bad drama lesson;
- it helps with motivation, as a way of celebrating good work or behaviour;
- it expands horizons – world music proves there is more to recorded sound than Lady Gaga;
- it can tap into learners' likes and values – youth culture and music are such close allies;
- it improves memory.

With so much going for it, I am still surprised by how little music is used in classrooms. When teachers do come to me and 'confess' that they have been using music in their lessons, it is almost as if a great burden has been taken from them, the reassurance that they are neither mad nor unprofessional, the relief that it's OK! I make it my personal mission to decriminalise the use of music in learning. It is OK, honest: not all the time, but when used in a balanced and professional way, with different music for different purposes, thought through and constantly evaluated for effect, yes, it's more than OK, it's crucial.

An easy experiment to try is to play Baroque largos from time to time in your classroom. Why? Research in the 1960s, by the godfather of accelerated learning Dr Georgi Lozanov, showed that they help us into the alpha brainwave configuration, ideal for learning – relaxed but awake. It's the same state, Lozanov noticed, in which Eastern yogis used to achieve feats of 'super-memorisation', except that they used relaxation and meditation. Listening to, for example, Bach's *Goldberg Variations* (think of the nice piano bit from the film *The English Patient*) or Pachelbels's *Canon for Strings and Bass in D* has the same effect on us. I once was doing a particularly noisy and active session with a group of 'disaffected and troublesome' boys, yet as soon as the exercise had finished I sent them off to write up what they had been doing with such music playing. Immediately, the energy levels in the room changed as these boys sat down to write. From noisy phys-ical to almost silent cerebral in a matter of seconds: it can be done.

For some, such a wanton recommendation of the use of music in learning is akin to blasphemy. Some people think the only way to learn is in complete silence. We call these people 'parents'. Yet research has shown that for some, complete silence is the last thing that they need in order to be able to concentrate effectively. The silence puts them under too much pressure, the stress starts to get to them and before you know it they have gone reptilian on you. Or else, the aural equivalent to such a wide-open space means their minds start to wander and they drift off from the task in hand.

'Musical wallpaper.'

A music video by Natalie Imbruglia on MTV, as described by journalist Michael J. Wolf in *Wired* magazine to explain how the channel was used harmlessly by students doing their homework. Now that's what I call chintz!

As with so many aspects of learning and motivation, variety is the watchword here. There is a need for silence in the classroom in the same way that there are learners in the classroom who have a need for music. Young people should, I feel, learn to be comfortable with silence because it is part of learning to be comfortable with oneself. Yet there is also a need for music for the many reasons already stated. Build opportunities for both into your classroom experiences and I am sure you will all benefit from the added richness it brings.

'Learning is experiences reflected on in tranquillity.'

William Wordsworth on the need for space to wander about on your own to think.

And remember, too, we are talking about music in its broadest sense, from an ambitious turning a project about the rainforest into a musical, to rapping the criteria for the relocation of industry (yes, it can be done), to chanting and clapping out scientific principles like football chants ('Stand up if you hate a vacuum'), to simply tapping out a rhythm as you reiterate a grammatical rule ('the "e" on the end makes long, long, long', tapped out on the table to remember the rule of the silent 'e' at the end of words such as like or fate). Even swapping the words from well-known songs or nursery rhymes with the information you are learning will do the trick ('Mary had a plebiscite … ').

And if you are ever stuck for inspiration when it comes to the use of such strategies for your lessons, go and visit a good languages lesson in which you will most probably experience the full gamut of musical tactics in use. If you have come across the work of former primary head, Sir Dave Winkley, a Birmingham-based pioneer in pushing the boundaries of what primary schools should be like, you will know that the teacher who helped his children pass their GCSE maths *while still at primary school* was not a maths teacher but a specialist in modern foreign languages.

Verbal/linguistic

Debates, stories, discussions, poems, essays, word games, synonyms and antonyms, rhyming words, radio commercials, slogans for tee shirts, marketing posters, speeches, diary entries.

Here we arrive back on safe ground for the traditionalists amongst you. We're back in IQ territory where logical/mathematical intelligence has to be expressed in a verbal/linguistic way and if you can't express it, you ain't got it.

> 'According to Plato, Socrates said writing was inhuman as it describes outside the mind what can only take place inside the mind. 'Writing destroys memory; those who use it,' Plato has Socrates argue, 'will become forgetful, relying on an external source for what they lack in internal resources. Writing weakens the mind.'
>
> Steven Rose, in *The Making of Memory* – think spellcheck!

Notice, though, the reference to *verbal* intelligence here, not simply linguistic intelligence. Can you think of any students – possibly some boys – who would have done a whole lot better in their exams if they only had to *tell* someone what they knew as opposed to writing it down neatly? Our brains have spent many millions of years learning without written communication. Indeed, writing is a very recent invention in human development, not to mention spelling. Even Shakespeare didn't know how or didn't care to spell his name consistently.

> 'He is an agonisingly slow writer with poor spelling and grammar.'
>
> A description of the man behind *Star Wars*, George Lucas, in the magazine *Eurobusiness*, reminding us that it takes more than the literacy hour to help us feel 'the force'.

The playwright Willy Russell resented the way that the working classes into which he had been born were considered intellectually inferior because they had a tradition of dealing in the spoken word, leading to conflict in the classroom. This was one of the reasons for him to turn from teaching to writing plays.

So, apart from building in time for plenty of class discussion, debate, argument (remember, for boys, this can mean confrontation, interruption, shouting, animal noises and abuse; it's natural and has been going on in parliament for hundreds of years), think also in terms of word games, diary entries, radio commercials, even poems. One school I worked with showed me how one girl was now using poetry in order to help her remember key concepts. This is her poem from Science on the rusting process:

> *Rusting*
> Rusting is a process that tries to ruin iron
> By chipping it and wearing it and never stops tryin'
> For rusting to happen it needs water and air
> Coz nothing will happen without those things there
> Rusting, rusting where should I begin?
> I'm gonna tell you how rusting can win
> It's not a contest, it's not a race
> Just how to stop rusting a very slow pace
> Just cover the iron with paint or zinc
> Coz that'll stop air and water getting in.
>
> *Naomi Philips*

Now, poetry may not be everybody's cup of tea but it worked for her. I disliked Science but if I had had the opportunity, from time to time, to record what I was learning in the style of a poem or a limerick, I know I would have risen to the occasion and probably still remember what I had learned to this day. Perhaps not all the time but some of the time (remember the watchword 'variety'), and some of the time would have been enough to help with my learning and with my motivation for learning.

Naturalistic

Going into the environment to learn, looking for links to nature, classifying into family groups, mathematical shapes in nature.

Remember the boy poacher from Chapter 1? Is his an example of an individual with high naturalistic intelligence? Do teachers sit at the back? It's a real-life *Kes* story.

And in your classroom? Is there that boy who hardly says a word to you but spends a great deal of time talking to his dog when he gets home, or the girl struggling with English but not with her pony? Naturalistic intelligence seems to stretch from the illiterate farmers and poachers of the world to the likes of Charles Darwin and Jacques Cousteau, taking in a whole range of vets, RSPCA inspectors, forestry workers and bird watchers along the way.

When I give teachers the task of coming up with classroom ideas for the whole range of intelligence areas during my INSET sessions it seems to be this one that throws up the most blank faces, and I must admit it is not obvious at first glance. Yet when you start to use that teacher's imagination and creativity of yours, you will be amazed at what comes up.

For a start, what are the chances of taking the class into the environment in order to learn? I know that if I am looking for inspiration the last thing I do is sit at my desk. I will go and take my dog for a walk in the countryside. Again, I know there are implications here for school life. One teacher I met at a secondary school told me how she used to take a troublesome class outside for their Science lessons, where she found they worked far better than inside, only to be prevented from doing so by the school management, as other classes had been asking to go out too. While I understand this is an issue, I also know that with a bit of imagination and determination there are ways of getting around it rather than resorting to such a blanket ban.

It also involves taking the time to consider your lessons through the eyes of someone who loves all things natural, from the smallest plants and animals to the landscapes of this and – perhaps – other worlds. For example in English, imagine the scenario whereby Disney ('It's a Disney world, we just live in it!') are about to do an animated version of *Macbeth*. Which animals would play the various characters, and why? I know one English teacher who did this exercise with her A-level English class and was given a real insight into the misinterpretation of the characterisation in *The Merchant of Venice* by some of her students. ('In tonight's performance the part of Shylock will be played by the Andrex puppy.') The same strategy can be used in History; this time the cartoon is about the First World War or the history of the American West or the Egyptians instead. And, talking of wars, what are the natural – as opposed to the political or historical – reasons for such conflicts? Could you consider persecution of other human beings through Darwinian eyes? Or what about the effect of the natural world on battles – or vice versa? (The great Edwardian short-story writer Saki – H. H. Munro – wrote a piece entitled *Birds on the Western Front*, detailing from first-hand experience the effect of the fighting on the wild birds of the region.) Even the story of Emily Davison throwing herself in front of the King's horse could be recounted though the eyes of the horse, another member of the community oppressed in order to serve man, perhaps? Through the eyes of the creatures living – and dying – in this environment? Or could your lesson on the family in French be about a family of dogs or cats or rabbits? Or even the discovery of mathematical shapes in nature – or should it be the other way around – how could this be interpreted differently? Did you know, for example, that, according to David Jones (in *Almost Like a Whale*?):

> [M]easurements of dozens of real rivers, and computer simulations of many more, show that the relationship between the shortest possible path across a plain and their actual length is always the same. It is pi, the ratio between the circumference of a circle and its diameter. Each river, whatever its size, goes a little more than three times further than it needs on its way to the sea.

There's one to drop into the conversation next time it goes quiet in the snug, as they say (although my personal favourite for the pub is Jones' claim that some birds increase the volume of their testicles by a hundred times in the spring).

A radio programme I heard a while back was profiling the UK's school farms. When it was first broadcast there were around a hundred or so of them but, following various challenges to their existence including the catastrophic foot-and-mouth disease outbreak in 2001 numbers dwindled to a low of sixty-six. At last count, I'm pleased to say, schools are refinding their passion for them and in 2012 there are eighty-two with more in the pipeline. The programme featured interviews with students, many of whom were boys, who, in a traditional school setting, had been disaffected and poorly behaved lads. After becoming involved with their school's farm, however, they had become engaged and motivated, not just for farm work but across the entire school. The programme also mentioned the work of the organisation known as The Countryside Foundation for Education which, according to its website – countrysidefoundation.org.uk – seeks to 'show how countryside issues can be used in a creative and often innovative way' and offers teaching materials across various key stages and for many curriculum areas.

Again, as I mentioned, I disliked Science and when pushed opted for Physics at O-level rather than Biology, yet I was an avid naturalist who could then – and still now – tell you a great deal about the natural history of the UK, especially from an ornithological perspective.

At the end of the day, we are natural beings living in a natural world and so tapping into all things naturalistic should not be too much of an obstacle if we apply ourselves to overcoming the artificial world that is school.

You will have spotted that you are already using some of the intelligences from the range anyway. Pat yourself on the back, if this is the case, and be aware of what you are doing well. Now make sure too that you are seeking to incorporate the areas that you aren't touching yet. Be aware too that we tend to teach according to the way that we prefer to learn. Just because, say, music is not your thing, does not mean that you should exclude it from your classroom as it could well be the 'thing' of at least one person in the class. Not only that, but one of the main ideas behind multiple intelligence work is to teach to the whole child and not just a narrow portion of the overall potential. Through multiple intelligence work we can play to strengths and build on weaknesses – ours as well as theirs.

Yes, certain intelligence areas fit better with certain subject areas. However, saying that Mozart has his chance to do music on a Thursday afternoon, so that's him happy, is not enough. Put that creative thinking hat on. How can you incorporate music into science and science into music? Now, in the 'real world', incorporating all eight areas into every lesson may appear a tad daunting. However, what you can do is to look at your schemes of work. Are there opportunities to work to these different intelligences incorporated across the term/topic/module? Apart from allowing students to work in their 'flow' state from time to time in a particular lesson, incorporating the different intelligences in this way has three big benefits:

1   It gives learners the chance to show the teacher just what they can do and, in doing so, they can change the teacher's expectations. And when those expectations have been changed then all sorts of things can happen.

Expectations and the report card

Many schools have a report card system for students with persistent behaviour issues. Whenever I have a student come to me with a report card at the beginning of the lesson, I write 'Excellent' on it and hand it straight back. I have never had to change what I wrote on the report card and every teacher to whom I have mentioned this has fed back to me that it works all the time.

There is so much research about children rising to our level of expectation, yet how are we making those expectations explicit? Sometimes we look at children as they walk through the door with that 'uh oh, here comes trouble' look. One friend of mine was virtually written off the moment he arrived at his upper school because of the behaviour of his elder brothers. As Goethe once said,

> If I accept you as you are, I will make you worse; however if I treat you as though you are what you are capable of becoming, I help you become that.

2   It gives children the chance to show their peers what they can do. In this way a child who perhaps never gets the chance to be 'part of the team' in, say, a Science lesson now has the opportunity for social inclusion because the task is to do a rap in science and he's good with music.

3   It gives students the chance to show themselves what they can do. This can only have a positive effect on self-esteem with all the positive rewards that that brings with it.

Three things you should know about self-esteem

The best definition of self-esteem I have come across is a two-part definition. To have high self-esteem you need to feel (a) capable and (b) loveable. And you need to feel both, one alone is not enough.

'I am good and I am able.'

Two key elements of Conducive Education, as opposed to feeling no good and being told you're less able, in what could be called coercive education.

Go up to a child in your class and ask them, on a scale of one to ten, with ten being top and one being bottom, how capable do they feel right now? Do they feel that there is a challenge in front of them at which they can succeed if they apply themselves (i.e. 10/10), or do they feel that even if they did try hard, they would fail anyway, so what's the point of even bothering in the first place (i.e. 1/10)? One strategy a headteacher told me about was to get a girl to write down three things she was good at on a slip of paper just before she was about to go and be told off. During the disciplinary process she was told to squeeze the paper harder and harder to remind her just what she was really capable of.

Are you aware that you cannot really raise anybody's self-esteem above your own? What are your levels of self-esteem like as an individual, as a member of staff, as a professional? Someone once likened it to the situation on an aeroplane with the oxygen masks. If you are travelling with babies and young children you are asked to put your own on first when needed.* Then, and only then, can you be of use to the children. It's an idea that Charles Handy refers to as 'proper selfishness'. Are you properly selfish? Do you take the time to look after yourself in order to be able to look after others? If you don't, you must.

> 'Switch off before you leave.'
>
> Sign below the light switch in a staffroom in Gloucestershire, to which someone had added: 'We try, we try!'

And thirdly, be aware that you cannot really raise someone's self-esteem for them, as it is not yours to raise in the first place, hence the word 'self'. All you can do is to work to create an environment in which their capability and love-ability starts to come through. Looking to incorporate

---

* And then choose your favourite …

opportunities for teaching through multiple intelligences helps with this aim. (As do simple ideas that we all know but so often forget, such as focusing not on the child – 'you naughty girl!' – but on the behaviour – 'That was a naughty thing to do!', focusing not on the present – 'Why are you always late?' but on the future – 'What are you going to do to make sure you get to school on time from now on?')

The use of multiple intelligences in the classroom also allows students to play 'in the zone' from time to time, as it affords them the opportunity to learn using their optimum learning state when learning is effortless and the living is easy. Mozart using music as a tool for learning in Science from time to time means that he has the chance to learn in his flow state at these times. Mozart never having the opportunity to use music in science means that he will always be outside his flow state in Science – in his 'anti-flow' if you like. Science will always be an effort and, although not impossible, it will never seem to come easily.

Another way of accessing this high-challenge, low-stress state is through deadlines – 'You have three minutes/thirty seconds/ who can be the quickest … ' And targets – 'See how many answers you can come up with/who will be the first to come up with ten answers'.

Working in this way also has some powerful positive effects on the workings and structure of the brain, as well as contributing towards maintained levels of creative thinking. To explain, let me take you back to neuroscience and a truism from the discipline.

Cells that fire together wire together

In other words, the more you use certain connections the stronger those connections become. For example, if I were to ask you to name a large, grey animal you might say – as would the majority of people asked, for a reason that statistics show but don't explain – elephant. The input enters your head and works its way through to the language processing centres in your brain causing connections to fire which lead to your output 'elephant', all in the blink of an eye. By leaving it at that, all we have managed to do is to reinforce your 'elephant' response to that question, meaning that there is even more likelihood that the next time you are asked the same question you will come up with the same response. But, what it also means is that there is less likelihood of ever coming up with other responses, as the corollary to the above truism is as follows:

When cells fire apart wires depart

Not as catchy, it's true, but a neurological verity all the same. If we don't use cells then the brain can, at best, reallocate them or, at worst, kill them off. This is a process known as 'neural pruning' or 'neural Darwinism', the brain ridding itself of what it doesn't need through the natural apoptosis. In *Brain Story*, Susan Greenfield describes how babies born with cataracts can remain blind even after having the cataracts removed in later life. The connections for seeing were not being used as the brain 'explored' what it needed and didn't need, so they were 'pruned away'. Are we born, then, with the potential to do anything? Everything? Gifted and talented guru David George sees it as follows:

> It seems to me that at birth nearly everyone is programmed to be outstanding. By the environment we provide, we change not just the behaviour of children but we change them at a cellular level.

Perhaps secondary schools should be having parents' evenings for parents of newborn children to save everyone a great deal of heartache over the coming sixteen years or so. The first three years of life are considered by many to be a real window of opportunity for stimulating many parts of the growing brain. That said, even in the womb the lifestyle and health of the mother can have implications for development of the child's brain (underweight babies have been shown to often develop learning difficulties, and high levels of stress experienced by the mother at a key time during pregnancy can lead to hyperactivity of the child later on – but only, apparently, if it is a boy).

By encouraging this infernal game of 'guess what's in the teacher's head' we are working to limit the creative integrity of our learner's brains. Or, put another way, *the more right we are the less flexible we become.*

Take that last sentence and pin it up in your staffroom. Teachers have spent a lifetime being 'right', but it can be a dangerous thing because they can lose sight of the vaguest possibility of other possibilities if they are not careful. Not just teachers, I know (send a copy of the sentence to your local MP while you are at it), but it seems that teachers, more than ever, are living a life that revolves around being right, having the set answers and knowing the score.

So, back to our classroom – rather than phrasing the question in a single-answer 'convergent' style try a multiple-answer, 'divergent' process, such as 'You have thirty seconds, name as many large, grey animals as you can', or 'Which table can be the quickest to come up with ten large, grey animals'. This way you can start with the easiest one such as 'elephant' – and, by the way, boys, especially, tend to be adept at lunging at the first and easiest answer that comes into their heads, which means that they can stop thinking after 1.6 seconds and then mess around, a process that also means that the more reflective female-type brains miss out on answering our questions – and then remain on task for the remaining 28.4 seconds as you consider more creative possibilities such as hippo, rhino, whale, narwhal, big donkey … And, on the subject of boys, notice the competitive element to the way this task is set. Such an exercise, set not all the time but some of the time, works to motivate the male brain. At other times you may want to make it non-competitive: 'Let's see how many the whole class can come up with by adding each table's scores together', or 'Let's find the three largest grey animals for each continent'.

Working in this way also has the added benefit of making sure that the learners have a little longer to answer a question than usual, which some research puts at as little as three seconds. Research also shows that when we do wait after asking a question, or after a child has answered, the child will then go on to respond in a more meaningful and extended manner.

In other words

- Give challenges with deadlines and targets.
- Actively seek to value all students.
- Incorporate multiple intelligences into your schemes of work, including teaching outside your own comfort zone from time to time.
- Break up your lessons.
- Be divergent in your thinking as well as convergent.
- Ensure a high self-esteem environment for all.
- Be explicit about high expectations.

Chapter 3

Mission control

According to the planet's leading authority on being happy, the definition 'that comes as close to what is usually meant by happiness as anything else we can conceivably imagine' is this one:

A sense of participation in determining the content of life.

In other words, we can be happy to the extent to which we *perceive ourselves to be* in control of our own lives. This is the view of our friend Mr Csikszentmihalyi, and I recommend that you have another look at the ideas in his book *Flow*, as I had to the first time I came across it. What are the implications in your classroom of such a revelation? Could it possibly be that there are children misbehaving in our classrooms because they want their happiness back? Csikszentmihalyi suggests that 'much of what we call juvenile delinquency ... is motivated by the need ... to have the flow experience not available in ordinary life'. Is that boy throwing that rubber at his friend on the other side of the room doing so because it is the only thing he feels he has control over ('It's not my fault Miss, it's my existential search for the state of flow.') in an environment in which he is told what to do, when to do it, how to do it but, quite possibly, never why to do it?

Csikszentmihalyi suggests that 'seeking pleasure is a reflex response built into our genes for the preservation of the species'.

The more we enjoy eating the more we are likely to eat and prosper. The more we enjoy sex, the more we are likely to eat and prosper. Think of it from the survival angle. Pleasure has been shown to improve our immune system. The more we laugh, the longer we live. Because of this we will consistently look for ways to take control of our lives and take our happiness back. In the classroom, this could be by seeking to do our very best if we perceive there to be a point (even if that point is merely one of enjoyment), or perhaps by aiming to sabotage the lesson to satisfy our own needs, a situation for which we may end up in trouble – but at least we are in control.

> 'A light heart lives long.'
>
> Shakespeare combining psycho-neuroimmunology with alliteration in *Love's Labours Lost*.

By considering what is regarded as poor behaviour as the result of a natural drive for happiness and survival we are further highlighting the need to focus on causes, not effects, in the classroom. Once we know the goal – in this case, to be happy by taking control – we can better understand the behaviours and do something constructive about them. Indeed, Pinker suggests that we would be foolish to describe a being as clever or otherwise without knowing their personal goals and intentions. He says, 'Without a specification of a creature's goals, the very idea of intelligence is meaningless', quoting the notion from cognitive scientist Zenon Pylyshyn that 'rocks are smarter than cats because rocks have the sense to go away when you kick them'.

The more I spend time with young people in schools the more I am coming to understand that for some students it takes a very particular sort of 'smart' to go through the school system and come out with no qualifications whatsoever. So, if the pursuit of the goal to be happy by taking control of my life by throwing the rubber at my friend is more pressing to my mind than cerebral application in the pursuit of a distant (and, when you're fourteen, three weeks seems distant) GCSE qualification-type goal, then the former will take precedence over the latter.

How are we to overcome this? Go back to the notion of humans as teleological, goal-focused beings, a concept known as 'psycho-cybernetics', described in a seminal book (*Psycho-Cybernetics – A New Way to Get More Living Out of Your Life*) by former plastic surgeon Maxwell Maltz. Look again at Chapter 1 in this book. If intelligence is the ability to narrow the gap between the current state of affairs and a desired future one, then the more we can make the desired one the socially acceptable and jointly agreed one (for example, working towards achieving the GCSE as a stepping-stone to a fulfilled life, and not throwing the rubber for a quick and fleeting burst of happiness), then the more we will be looking at internally motivated learners in our classrooms.

Delayed gratification and the marshmallows

There is a famous test, in psychological circles if not in confectionery ones, in which young children in the 1960s were tested for how well they could delay the gratification of eating marshmallows. It is recounted in detail in Goleman's *Emotional Intelligence*, and the results of what was discovered are significant when we look at the need to teach young people to take control of their lives, including their feelings and compulsions.

The children who were unable to resist their impulses to eat marshmallows in the experiment were, during their adolescent years:

> more likely to be seen as shying away from social contacts; to be stubborn and indecisive; to be easily upset by frustrations; to think of themselves as 'bad' or unworthy; to regress or become immobilised by stress; to be mistrustful and resentful about not

'getting enough'; to be prone to jealousy and envy; and to overact to irritations with a sharp temper. And they were still unable to put off the desire for a quick fix.

If you think that makes a compulsive reason for making sure that you practise the art of delayed gratification in your classroom, especially with younger children, just wait until you see how the group of children who were able to delay gratification turned out. In their teens this second group were 'more socially competent', not to mention:

> personally effective, self assertive and better able to cope with the frustrations of life ... less likely to go to pieces, freeze or regress under stress, or become rattled and disorganised when pressured; they embraced challenges and pursued them instead of giving up, even in the face of difficulties; they were self reliant and confident, trustworthy and dependable; and they took the initiative and plunged into projects.

And if that wasn't enough, it gets better:

> According to their parents' evaluations, they were more academically competent, better able to put their ideas into words, to use and respond to reason, to concentrate, to make plans and follow through on them, and more eager to learn.
>
> (Goleman, *Emotional Intelligence*, 1996)

The difference between those who grabbed marshmallows and those who waited most astonished Goleman when he looked at their combined average SAT scores for maths and English. The delayers of pleasure were outperforming the others by a massive 210 points, leading Goleman to point out that, at the age of 4, this simple marshmallow test is a far better predictor of children's future SAT scores than an IQ test.

Unless the researchers had inadvertently discovered some amazing benefits of increasing marshmallow intake at age 4, what comes through loud and clear is that we, as teachers, need to be working with children to help them learn to understand and be master of their impulses and not the other way round. This, for me, is the essence of emotional intelligence – the identification and understanding of our emotions and the ability to work with them consciously to achieve our goals.

Back at the control room, what makes this whole process of passing control over to the students easy is the fact that this sense of control need only be that, a sense of control. You, the teacher, are not throwing your entire classroom, lesson plans and professional career over into the hands of the students. What you are doing is working in such a way that they at least feel they are in control of what is happening, co-authors of their school career and not, at best, the passive passengers on the journey or, at worst, the victims of some terrible process.

A piece of research I once heard about entailed two groups of volunteers who were put in separate booths, played high-volume music and monitored for the effects of stress by observing aspects such as heartbeat and blood pressure. One of the groups had only the music. The others were given what they were told was a volume control. Monitoring of their responses showed that the group without the volume control had stress levels that were going through the roof. However, the group with the volume control had responded less dramatically, even though the volume control *was not actually attached to anything and had no effect on the volume of the music*. What the researchers had identified was that it is not control that makes the difference but the sense of control, a perception that we are having a direct influence on our lives.

In the classroom this can be something as simple and straight-forward as asking the class whether they want to do task A or task B first. You have not lost any of your overall control – you are the one setting up both tasks and you are the one offering them to your class – but you are allowing the students to make a choice, to take control.

According to Eric Jensen in his book *Completing the Puzzle: The Brain-Based Approach*, 'Choice changes the chemistry of the brain.' When we are given – and take – choices about what to do and the way to do it the brain ends up in a far better chemical state than when we are told what to do. Choice and control lead to lower stress levels and encourage the release of endorphins which consist of, among other things, the 'pleasure' neurotransmitters dopamine and serotonin. However, take the control away and instead the brain will generate a different neurotransmitter – noradrenaline – which closes down our thinking, leading to low morale, poor learning and reduced motivation. All this can result from something as simple as allowing them to choose which one of the five questions on the board they want to start with, as opposed to making them all start at number 1 and go on to number 5; or by asking them if they want to do their timed essay at the beginning of the lesson or at the end of the lesson; or whether that boy would like to take his baseball cap off or get into trouble (and then walk away as he makes his mind up).

> 'All authority is quite degrading. It degrades those who exercise it and degrades those over whom it is exercised. When it is violently, grossly or cruelly used, it produces a good effect, by creating, or at any rate bringing out, the spirit of revolt.'
>
> Oscar Wilde writing in *The Soul of Man Under Socialism* about how we can put our foot down only to shoot ourselves in it.

Have you ever seen the trick in which a fifty-pence piece 'walks' across the back of someone's fingers? I once saw a tramp doing it in Leicester Square, dexterously flipping the coin backwards and forwards across the back of his hand by simple movements of his fingers. To do such a trick – and I believe twirling batons is similar – you have to let go of the object you are manipulating, yet you retain control throughout the exercise. It is the momentum you have set up that carries you through. Think of teaching in the same way.

Teacher as hypnotist

Whether you believe in hypnosis or not, all teachers need to be aware of the power of the language that they use and the effects – good and bad – of the words they are firing off like so many loose cannons throughout their teaching careers.

During my INSET events I ask delegates to raise their hands if they are poor singers. Many often do, often the majority, like some great anti-choir. I then ask an individual how he or she knows they can't sing. Nine times out of ten they have been told by someone else, and while that might have been a recent event (a family member hammering on the bathroom door, for example) the first time that it happened usually turns out to have been at school – 'Can you mime please, you're putting the pianist off '. One teacher explained how she had been told to be a 'hummingbird' in the school choir and had to stand on the edges of the choir and hum rather than join in with gusto.

'There is no such thing as an un-musical person. Tone deaf are simply people who were told as children not to sing for fear of "spoiling the choir" and carry that negative conversation with them ever since.'

Top conductor and management guru Benjamin Zander on why you have more power in your little

> finger than 100 advertising copywriters. Zander
> refers to himself as a 'relentless architect of the
> possibilities of human beings'. Next time someone
> at a party asks what you do, tell them that. It's true
> and it's so much better than pretending you sell
> insurance.

When I ask those who are musical to raise their hands, and ask them if they think the 'non-singers' could improve, the answer is always, Yes. Yet, the message that burrowed into the subconscious mind of the 'non-singers' as children is that they could not – and never would be able to – sing. In the subconscious, this belief – coming as it does from a figure of knowledge and authority, a teacher, therefore it must be true, because a teacher wouldn't lie, would they, and they always know best, in fact they always know everything – takes root in our self-concept. From then on in, it becomes an unchallenged self-fulfilling truth. Yet it simply isn't true.

I heard once about a tribe in Africa in which everyone can play a variety of instruments and sing by the age of four. Learning to play an instrument is as natural to them as learning to speak or walk. It is as inconceivable to them that a healthy child should not be musical as it is for us to have a perfectly fit and healthy child who is unable to walk.

I then repeat the exercise but this time refer to drawing ability – again the same response. (And for those of you who want to draw better check out a book called *Drawing on the Right Side of the Brain* by Bettie Edwards. Instead of using the 'wrong' bits of the brain to draw, namely the language-biased left hemisphere, she shows you how to use the 'right' side which deals better with shapes, forms, spaces, contrast, texture, rhythm, and is, on the whole, a far better amateur artist.)

There are some other benefits of looking at the language of choice. Take the straightforward question:

Do you want your test before break or after break?

Built into this simple sentence is a powerful linguistic tool referred to as a presupposition. This is the element in a sentence or question that is not up for grabs and enters our subconscious mind unchallenged. It is a very potent tool and a key element in the hypnotist's arsenal. I once heard media hypnotist Paul McKenna describing some of the processes he used for his stage act. The questions he uses such as, 'Have you ever been hypnotised before?' carry forceful presuppositions that allow him to work very quickly and effectively with hilarious results (if you find people pretending to be dishwashers hilarious).

The WYSIWYG brain

There was a time when what you saw on the computer screen was not what came out of the printer. Then came the WYSIWYG (What You See Is What You Get) program. Our minds work in the same way – what you focus on, on an on-going basis, is what you end up with. People in the staffroom who are always complaining about being ill, are always ill: and so are the people who listen to them. You can catch a cold over the phone. I am rarely the only individual in an INSET session who left school thinking, 'I don't know what I want to do, but I don't want to become a teacher'. What is the focus of National No Smoking Day? It's the one day in the year when people who don't smoke spend the day thinking about cigarettes ('Mmmm, I wonder what all this fuss is about … '). Recently it was on Ash Wednesday. Your diet won't last long if you spend your days thinking about cakes. Bear in mind this WYSIWYG principle when you are talking to young people. A conversation that focuses on the child always being late is unlikely to be as productive as a conversation on punctuality.

'Anti-religious sentiment quickened his interest in religion.'

Louis Fischer describing the effect a campaign of 'Just Say No' to religion had on the young Gandhi in his biography of the great man. Related to this is the notion that the subconscious mind does not hear the word 'don't'. As a waiter in a restaurant, I knew that the surest way of getting a punter to touch a red-hot plate was to ask him or her not to touch it. Remember that next time you say to children, 'Don't be late … ', 'Don't forget your homework … ', 'Don't take drugs … '.

Once we become aware of presuppositions, we need to make sure we are using them for good and not for evil. For example, what are the presuppositional differences between the following two similar but very different sentences?

Those of you who finish can go and do the poster work.

When you finish you can go and do the poster work.

The presupposition in the first one is very clear – 'some of you are going to finish and some of you aren't. I know who you are and you know who you are so go ahead and fail. That's OK because that's what we are all expecting, isn't it?' Evidence that, as Freud once said, 'We bleed our beliefs through every pore.' In the second sentence, the presupposition changes to one in which the implication is that everyone has the same potential for completion of the task, which is a far more powerful starting point for a lesson. I know, in reality, that some will finish faster than others, yet at least in the second sentence everyone starts off on an equal footing and certain students are not written off before they have even begun.

It's a simple strategy that, once you become aware of how you are using language, has many different uses at work ('Do you want to do the extra bus duty today or on Friday?', 'Which of your free periods would you be most happy to lose?') and at home ('Would it be best for you if I went to the pub before you made tea or afterwards?' – count the presuppositions in there!). I found it to be a very useful tool for working with my own children (I have three, so I may as well experiment on them). 'Would you like your story while you're in bed or before you go to bed?' was a good time-for-bed-type question. It works from a very young age, too, as I found with my youngest daughter. As soon as she was able to understand language I was able to say to her, to 'help' her stop crying unnecessarily, 'Do you want to sit and cry on the stairs or stay here and smile?' Nine times out of ten she would respond with the start of a smile, and the drama – and the noise – would be over. If she did opt to sit on the stairs, I made it clear that she could come back in as soon as she had stopped crying; it was her choice to go there and it was her choice when she came back round again. This helped me avoid the often meaningless, 'Go to your room until I tell you to come out,' scenario, in which either they sneak back down later and so erode another brick from the wall of your ability to discipline your children, or else you forget about them.

In a primary school, once, a boy was misbehaving in my lesson. I gave him the choice to behave like his friends or sit apart from the group. He chose the former yet after a few minutes he started misbehaving again so I asked him to sit on his own. He stomped off and hid himself behind a table and, although the teacher in me wanted to scream something along the lines of 'Sit where I can see you and look happy whilst I humiliate you,' I let him be. Within five minutes his head was popping out from behind the table and he gradually reintroduced himself into the lesson.

A sense of control through co-ordinated choices is a very, very powerful tool in the armoury of any parent or teacher and brings with it, I believe, many other benefits, not the least of which is what many observers believe to be the most important attitudinal trait that any individual searching for success can have – a sense of responsibility.

The very first time I came across any of the sort of information about the realisation of human potential was during a Diploma in Entrepreneurial Management that I was taking at Durham University Business School (it was the 1980s, we were young). The session in question was a day-long contribution to our entrepreneurial abilities and was entitled 'The Psychology of Success', which left many of us cold as no one had spoken about either of the main themes to any of us throughout our successful school and university careers. However, what this man introduced us to – and Mr Dobbins, may I publicly thank you – were some fundamental principles that would change my life.

'Make responsibility a part of your enjoyment.'

Small print in an American magazine advert for bourbon, reminding us to think like we drink.

'If the only thing I get across to you today,' said Mr Dobbins at one point, mid-way through the session, 'is that you are responsible for your own success, you will go far, and I will have achieved a great deal today.' It is a sentiment that I reiterate in my student events. Our real potential only starts to take off when we understand that achieving what we want is down to us – and us alone. We may – and indeed should – draw support from other people and their help in the struggle towards achieving our goals but, at the end of the day, whether we sink or whether we swim is down to us.

The great lie

During the session at the business school in Durham I realised for the first time that I had been taken in by the great lie – 'Do well at school, get a good job'. It may be

> true, but it doesn't mean you get to *keep* the good job. And
> what about all those people out there with fantastic jobs
> but no qualifications? There must be more to it. Looking
> back, I consider the secret of success at school for me was
> 'Wait to be told what to do and do it well.' What I know
> now is that it is better to work out what you want, cut out
> the waiting and go and do that well. Yet, the strategy that
> was successful at school could actually get in the way of
> success beyond school.

Writing in the now defunct *Sunday Business* in 1998, Ruth
Lea, then head of the policy unit at The Institute of Directors,
said this:

> The written assumption appears to be that a degree (any
> degree) from a university (any university) will inevitably
> make a person 'better educated' and more employable. But
> there is increasing evidence that this is not the case. Indeed,
> how could anyone have ever thought that this could be so? ...
> I believe there are groups of people going to university who
> are not helping their employability by studying for a degree.

Is your advice to that 16-year-old the best advice possible?
Do you have enough knowledge of life beyond school to offer
any advice at all? At school you went to the top by waiting to be
told what to do and doing it well, yet our man Mr Dobbins was
instructing me to cut out the waiting, work out what I wanted
and then go and do that well – 'If it's to be, it's up to me'. The
more I considered the nature of success the more I realised that
this sense of responsibility was at the heart of personal achievement. What's more, I began to realise that in many ways a stable
home and success in the education system could actually deny an
individual the opportunity to take up the challenge of responsibility, that success at school could actually prevent me from
achieving my potential beyond school.

Mr Dobbins described the principles of maturity and success through responsibility by likening it to the Grand Canyon. It went something like this. Imagine, then, the cross-section of this valley. On one side you have 'C' for child, on the other 'A' for adult. As a child you don't have to take responsibility for anything. Human beings have the longest period of childhood in the Animal Kingdom. Why? To answer that we have to go back to neurological evolution again. As our brains grew, evolution decreed that a fair proportion of the time the child's brain needed for its own development was going to have to be outside the womb. Apparently, if our bodies continued to grow at the same rate that our brains do after birth we would be ten feet tall and weigh about a tonne. The other alternative of giving birth to babies whose brains – and consequently heads – were the size of those of an adult was also deemed to be impracticable by Mother Nature, her eyes watering. The compromise was to extend beyond birth the maturation processes of the human brain, to on average about between twenty and thirty years after birth. This is the average age at which the human brain is fully wired up, ready to go and functioning at what we would call an adult level. Bear this in mind when you think about how we lump together a group of children because they have birthdays within set periods of time and then start to measure them one against the other. We are not comparing like with like, however, as there could well be a 3-year spread across the class between the different levels of brain development – not to mention that boys and girls develop different areas, and consequently different faculties, at different times.

'We know young people develop at separate ages. Why do we insist that they should all develop at the same pace?'

Charles Handy on the arbitrary nature of lumping children together because of their birth date.

During this extended period of childhood, a slow but steady process of transferring from dependent to independent should come into play until we leave the bosom of the family as fully-fledged, self-reliant adults. This has to be one of the most important roles of parenthood – not to mention one of the most difficult and heart-wrenching – the preparation of our offspring to live a life in which we are no longer of use to them. Kahlil Gibran puts it with his usual metaphysical eloquence: 'You are the bows from which your children as living arrows are sent forth.'

> 'My parents were wonderful in creating an environment that let me look at all the possibilities.'
>
> Bill Gates on why parents need to open up the world to their children and not hide them from it. A tutor told me recently that she had been asked not to encourage a girl in her ambition of being a travel rep. because her father insisted that she stay in her home town for the rest of her life.

It is this process, aeons old and highly successful as we have evolved, that John Abbott uses to show how counterintuitive the current education system really is. Genetics and evolution both push towards a process that goes from reliance to independence but, flying in the face of such evidence, we have an educational system which takes us in the completely opposite direction. In this system 5-year-olds are put in classes of thirty or more, with one adult to share between them, at the very time when the closer and more immediate the support from the adult the better. (Abbott suggests that the natural optimal group size for 6-year-olds is about ten.) Then, as they go through the system, at the very time they are naturally yearning for independence, we reduce the class sizes (think sixth-form teaching groups) and give them one-to-one tutorials and all sorts of other heavily prescriptive, responsibility-sapping processes. And, as John Abbott is not slow to point out to the cheers, I am sure, of all primary teachers in the audience, we all know at which age the learner attracts the most money from the state.

Returning to the Grand Canyon, however, we see that success comes from making it to the 'A' side of the chasm, the side of adulthood, which has nothing to do with age, voting rights or the sorts of videos you can legally rent but is all about your maturity as a responsibility-taking – as opposed to simply responsible – adult. This is the point we should be working towards in secondary schools, and beyond, if we are to take seriously our obligation to prepare young people to be all they can be in their lives beyond school.

Many teachers I speak to tell me how they are achieving success at GCSE but that for many students it is not transferring into success in the sixth form. When I ask why, they are always quick to admit the reason and the part they play in the situation: 'We spoon-feed them for GCSEs and then they don't know how to do it for themselves at A-level'. What is the drop-out rate or the change to fewer, even just easier, A-levels in your school if you have a sixth form? What are the levels of drop-out like at our colleges and universities? We have a system that rewards us for spoon-feeding our children and in doing so denies them the opportunities to take responsibility for their own success, and then we throw them into college or university and wonder why so many can't cope.

The big gap between child and adult on our Grand Canyon model is where things get interesting, a yawning chasm which Mr Dobbins referred to ominously as 'The Valley of Excuses'. This is littered with the frustrated dreams and desires of all those who don't make the leap between adult and child, recognised by their despairing wails of 'If only … !', 'I would have but … ' and 'It's alright for you … !' Here are the thousand-and-one excuses as to why an individual has tried and failed or, in many cases, not even tried at all. The war, the government, the teachers, the system, the parents, the economic climate – there is an excuse for every failed dream and unfulfilled aspiration (remember our underachieving students in Chapter 2).

'You're a "but" man. That's the difference between success and failure – the use of the word "but".'

Homer Simpson explaining the secret of success to neighbour Ned Flanders.

I learned very early on in my working life that – and I'm not one of those who like to classify people – there are essentially two sorts of human beings: DDMs and DMDs.

A DDM is a 'Don't Do: Moan'; they don't like what's going on but, rather than use their personal power to do anything about it, they will sit around whingeing about it, complaining how powerless they are and if they were in control, oh my, how things would be different. Huddled around the water coolers and tea trolleys of the working world, muttering in photocopier queues and staffrooms, grumbling into their mugs ('Hey, that's my mug!') of coffee, these are the could-have-been contenders of modern society. However, for every group of DDMs I have encountered I will always find at least one DMD.

A DMD is a 'Don't Moan: Do' and the DMDs are the ones quietly changing the world, putting right what they perceive to be wrong and using the power they have to take action and make a difference, not wasting their energies on blame and equivocation. DMDs can not only be found writ large in human history, from Saint Francis of Assisi to Martin Luther King, Albert Schweitzer to Bob Geldof, but also in the daily comings and goings of people on your street or in your local pub.

'Sometimes I would like to ask God why He allows poverty, famine and injustice to continue when He could do something about it … but I don't in case He asks me the same question.'

Readers' Digest wisdom on why we sometimes prefer the easy life in the Valley of Excuses.

One example, which I have come across quite often, relates to the differing individual responses to being faced with a situation such as redundancy. Where I have known some people to go to pieces over such a dilemma (remember your post is being made redundant, not you), others, once they have overcome the immediate and very real concerns and emotions, hang on to their personal responsibility and set out to make a better situation than the one they had in the first place. I have lost count of the number of successful entrepreneurs I have come across whose big break was their redundancy money and who, looking back, refer to losing their jobs as, 'The best thing that ever happened to me.'

> **'It was like being kicked in the ass with a golden horseshoe!'**
>
> **Arthur Black, co-founder of American DIY chain Home Depot, on being fired from his job at Handy Dan's Home Improvement Centers. You never know where the next golden horseshoe is going to hit.**

For further reinforcement of these principles just take apart the word 'responsibility' to make *response-ability*: our *ability* to *respond* to what is coming our way.

To what extent are we engineering opportunities for young people to learn and hone their ability to respond in this way? I have seen so many occasions when a teacher – with the very noblest of caring intentions – will jump in and 'rescue' a student from having to face the consequences of his or her actions. ('I'll do it for you but just this once', 'You can use my pen but can I have it back this time?'). I used to resent thoroughly the idea that I was the one supposed to make sure that a student who was too lazy to get out of bed to arrive at my lesson on time caught up on what he had missed. Working on the premise that what gets rewarded gets repeated, not only would I have been denying him the opportunity of having to face up to the consequences of his actions, I would also have been actually encouraging him to continue in his idle ways through the special attention and one-to-one teaching he was receiving. This is another example in which, for some students, *de*tention actually equates to *atten*tion. What they must realise at this point is that, if they continue to pursue a policy of academic mediocrity, then they are *choosing* to do so. It is a choice, a conscious one, that they are making, and they must be prepared to take between the eyes the consequences of their decisions.

As the teacher, tutor or mentor, try to avoid giving the choice a value – good or bad – but help them remember, by the language you use and encourage them to use, that it is *their choice* and, as such, can be changed at any point, either now or in the future. After all, 'Nothing is written,' as Peter O'Toole says to Omar Sharif (in *Lawrence of Arabia*) before hopping on a camel and taking Akabar from the rear.

There are times, however, when the slow adolescent climb towards emotional maturity and responsibility can be given a dramatic push, and a young individual is left with no choice but to sink or to take responsibility and swim. The loss of a parent or parents or, at the very least, the loss of the faculties of the parents has been the turning point for many a future successful career, the point at which these individuals learnt the hard way that, 'if it's to be, it's up to me'. Research into self-made millionaires at the University of Manchester Institute of Science and Technology (UMIST) identified that 'a disproportionate number of successful people have lost a parent, been rejected by a parent or have had a loss-related event before the age of 18', according to Professor Cary Cooper. And Howard Gardner in *Leading Minds*, a book on great leaders, identifies that '60 per cent of major British political leaders had lost a parent during childhood, mostly the father'. As Winston Churchill once said, 'Famous men are usually the product of an unhappy childhood.'

> 'Life became something I had to make up as I went along and I had to work everything out for myself.'
>
> James Dyson on the effect of losing his father when he was just 9 years old.

As a footnote to this chapter on taking responsibility and retaining control, think about your life as a teacher. Would you say you had an internal or an external locus of control? If you have this sense that everything is out of your control, then you are more likely to end up stressed and ill. By trying to control it all we end up out of control. One teacher I met was stressed all the time as he tried to 'get the job done' before he went home each night. Yet the job is such that it will never be 'done'. What he seemed to miss was, to give it a more polite description, a 'sod-it valve', that function in our brain that says, 'that's it, time to go!' By thinking in terms of yes/no, finished/unfinished, black/white, in control/out-of-control we set ourselves up to fail – or worse.

For a start, one of the best ways to be in control in the class-room is to give control. The more we try to control our class with a vice-like grip, the more some young people will find ways of subverting our best efforts. (Have you ever drunk in a JD Wetherspoon pub? They are named after a teacher that entrepreneur and founder of the chain Tim Martin had at school who couldn't control his class!) Yet control, like respect, is acquired in the giving of it. As Dr Stephen Covey says, 'Trust is the highest form of motivation.'

Second, research on eighty headteachers found that, of those who could only think in terms of black and white and became angry when crossed, 35.7 per cent had seen their GP in the last six weeks compared with only 6.7 per cent of their more flex-ible and tolerant fellow heads, who permitted shades of grey elements to enter their lives. Are you operating, in the words of the management at GE Capital, a 'loose–tight development process'?

The message to us all is that the job is always bigger than we are and that we keep control by realising that there are things we can control and things we can't (and hopefully knowing one from the other).

> 'There's only one corner of the universe that you can be certain of changing and that's your own.'
>
> Aldous Huxley on where our influence on the world starts.

So, control means choice and choice involves responsibility. What, then, are the opportunities for responsibility that you are offering students in your school? Suzie Hayman, who wrote a book for parents on coping with adolescents, suggests that 'one of the reasons adolescence is becoming so difficult is the failure of adults to give teenagers more responsibility', citing the case of the 15-year-old boy who felt that the only responsibility he had in his life was for his pencil!

An element of choice in the classroom does more than encourage responsibility and pander to the neurology of happy learning. It also links into the whole controversial area of learning styles and preferences and the claim that we do tend to learn best when we learn in a particular way that suits us at any given time. That's not to say we can't learn in other ways, ever, but it does seem to reflect the fact that, taking myself as an example, if I don't see it, it doesn't go in that well. Call it a style or a preference or what you will, the key message for any teacher to take from it isn't one of classification and pigeonholing but of variety. Give students a variety of ways of accessing the new knowledge and that – in and of itself – can help more of them learn more effectively and efficiently.

For example, taking the well-known VAK model (visual, auditory, kinaesthetic or, put simply, see the learning, hear the learning, do the learning), it's quite easy to prepare lessons that take all three on board on a regular basis.

'We do VAK in maths – children get to see the teacher, hear the teacher and watch him walking about!'

Comment overheard from a maths teacher who was, almost, only joking.

What is sometimes overlooked, though, is the order the VAK inputs come in. Show them the PowerPoint, talk them through it, do the practical is a common 'VAK-ed' lesson format that goes in exactly that order – see, hear, do. However, some people may prefer the complete opposite – do some practical work, talk about what happened, see the presentation to find out what it should have been like. Others still may prefer talking about it, seeing it and then doing it: variety within variety, if you like.

Some students – two or three in every thirty, according to Michael Grinder in *Righting the Educational Conveyor Belt* – face a real learning block when working outside their 'preference' and can tend to become derailed. A GP I was training once came to me after the session and recounted how he was not allowed to take A-levels at school because he was not 'clever enough' and had been forced to leave and go through a circuitous route via college to achieve the qualifications needed to pursue his ambition. Looking back, he realised that he was – and indeed still is – a predominantly kinaesthetic learner. I know the school that had denied him his place in the sixth form and know it to be not only the most successful secondary school in the county, by way of examination results, but also a very traditional school. For 'traditional' read 'sit down, shut up, books out, listen, then write'. In other words, it was an environment almost exclusively devoted to V and A strategies that not only denied the K students the opportunity to shine but also made them appear less able than the others. Persisting with his career plans, despite being written off by his school, the GP in question had discovered a new-fangled invention called a CD-ROM that would really allow him, he said, to 'get to grips' with his learning, taking the learning out of the auditorium and putting it into his own hands. He also scored highly during his medical training in one particular element of his course – dissection.

In a school in France one group of children was given 26 per cent less academic study time compared with what was normal, with the time left over being reallocated to physical activities such as swimming and gym. Apart from being reported to be more calm and attentive with fewer discipline problems, the 'test' group also fared exactly the same as the control ('normal') group in the 'certificate of study' tests. As concluded from a telling piece of educational research, 'physical education when taught correctly promotes the development of intellectual skills as well as motor skills.'

The GP's story is just one; there are countless others of people who are written off, when it comes to learning, by an ignorance in the classroom that decrees that there is one way to learn and those who don't get it haven't got it. Howard Gardner, of *Multiple Intelligences* fame, refers to this notion as the theory of 'one-chance learning'. If you don't learn first time, then you probably will never learn and, anyway, the curriculum says we have to move on. Whereas, as we found in Chapter 2, the use of multiple intelligences in the classroom impacts on our schemes of work; exploiting what we know about learning preferences demands that variety should be written into each and every lesson plan. And to make matters harder for the poor unfortunate souls with preferences that don't match the system, we tend to teach according to the way that *we* prefer to learn, the unspoken implication being, 'If it's good enough for me then what's wrong with you?'

The 'V-type' teacher will have an ever-changing array of display work and hand-written worksheets worthy of being framed. There is usually much use of visual sources, from books and handouts (and if they have to use photocopies, they may try for coloured paper) to magazines and videos. Students will be actively encouraged to use colour in their books and to record information in non-verbal ways such as through symbols and pictures. Poster work is a positive addition to students' learning. However, they may not be so good with storytelling and attracting attention or commanding respect through their voice. They may well dress in a dynamic way.

The 'A-type' teacher perhaps hasn't changed the displays since the 1930s. Visual resources may be scant and traditional ('Are these black and white photocopies a bit too gaudy?'), and poster work is encouraged from time to time because there is less marking that way. Yet they are powerful storytellers with variety of tonality and pitch in their voices which they use for engaging students and shouting down corridors. They may well dress in quite a drab sort of way, although men may wear a Wallace and Gromit tie.

The 'K-type' teacher is actually quite a rare phenomenon in a classroom (although not, of course, on a sports field or in a gym. A colleague of mine was attending a workshop a few years back when analysing teachers' learning styles was *de rigueur*. By far, the vast majority were visual or auditory, with only a tiny fraction showing a kinaesthetic preference. Yet, of this minority, nearly all were PE teachers or at least had been until their knees went). 'K-type' teachers may appear poorly organised and messy yet they have a way of developing a rapport with like-minded students (think underachieving boys) on a one-to-one level. And they have probably forgotten to get dressed properly at all.

Regardless of what you think about the learning styles controversy, do you systematically guarantee that there are opportunities for V, for A *and* for K during the course of each lesson? Why not try some of the following examples?

Some 'see the learning' strategies

Posters, pictures, colour co-ordinating learning, use of favourite colours, highlighter pens, Post-it® pads, Mindmaps*, video, flip cameras, cameras on their phones, computers, effective use of the interactive whiteboard, creative visualisation, watching role-plays or professional theatre, active reading strategies (for example, scanning for key facts in a timed situation – 'The answer to this question is on the sheet in front of you, you have thirty seconds to find it, raise your hand when you've got it, you can turn the sheets over … now!').

Visual memory strategies are useful here too, bearing in mind we have a limitless memory for pictures, especially weird and wacky ones. Check out any of the wealth of books on such strategies, and never let that little question 'How shall I learn this, Sir?' go unanswered again.

'It's not a matter of intelligence. Anyone can do this.'

Reassuring words from World Memory Champion Andy Bell, someone who left school at sixteen with no prospects and just four O-levels but spent four years training his brain using visual memory strategies.

Some 'hear the learning' strategies

Put the learning into your own words, simply tell someone else or, even better, teach someone else. Encourage students to record their learning on to their phones – again in their own words – and listen regularly. Research shows that just before sleeping and just after waking up are good times for reviewing material. Many professional actors see those two times as key when it comes to learning their lines. Also, make sure you are drawing on a medley of rhymes and rhythms, chants and songs, debates, discussions and dialogues. And remember to think about the music you are using in the classroom.

Some 'do the learning' strategies

Who says that sit down, back straight, legs crossed, arms folded, eyes front, big smile, look of love is the best position for learning? Looking at you may actually put me off learning because in order to concentrate I need to stare into space or out of the window. After all, as Dali said, 'To gaze is to think.' Do you doodle when you are in a lecture? Does it stop you learning? Of course not, so look for creative ways of letting your students fidget. I know of at least one primary school that allows children to doodle while listening to stories now.

Research has shown that some people learn better when they are walking up and down when reading. In one primary school I was told that years ago the head used to have the 'remedial kids' in the hall walking up and down as they read – and read well.

> 'I have walked myself into my best thoughts.'
>
> Søren Kierkegaard, Danish philosopher and theologian, proving that men can think and walk simultaneously (although chewing gum at the same time may prove to be too much).

Acting out the learning can range from whole-scale role-play (I once saw a video of a science teacher who would take his students into the playground to act out the process of molecules being heated up spinning ever faster and looser) to small-group work. Please note that we are not necessarily talking performance art here. Not every scenario has to be performed before the whole class. The process of having done it in small groups is enough for many students.

You can even encourage students to anchor the learning to their body and access their powerful 'muscle memory' – the memory built into the physical act of doing something such as riding a bike or remembering your cashpoint number.

> **'I have never forgotten the lesson you so kindly gave me: even my leg remembers it.'**
>
> Oscar Wilde, in a letter to a friend thanking them for a lesson in how to ride a bike, proving that his genius was not just in his head.

In one geography lesson a girl was having a great deal of trouble understanding what the teacher was going on about. She had had the information about coastal erosion in her ears (teacher at the front of the class), she had had it in her eyes (handout) but she had not yet grasped what the concepts meant. Her frustration was palpable and motivation at crisis point. However, by taking her through the terms in a physical way ('Rub the back of your hand with your finger. If you did that for the next fifty years what would happen? Well, that's erosion.' Then, 'Put your hands on the desk, thumbs up, fingertips touching. Now bend your fingers towards you. That's the bay, your two wrists are the headlands.'), you could see the penny drop. Once the information was 'in' she could then go on to explore the learning using, for example, multiple intelligences.

Here's another one from geography. Hold your hand up in front of you in a fist; now hold your hand up with your fingers together, thumb towards you; now hold up your hand with fingers spread wide. Then think 'settlements'. In the first explanation you have a physical – kinaesthetic – representation of a 'nuclear' settlement, in the second, it's a 'linear' one, and in the third, 'dispersed'. Again, these are physical ways of taking in key terms.

It's worth remembering at this point that we also have different sorts of memory and, for example, our memory for pictures is different from and separate to our memory for sounds, which is different again from our physical – or muscle – memory. Even verbs and nouns are stored in different parts of the brain, apparently. If all your students do is sit and read their books repeatedly for revision, then they are using one memory channel only. Yet when they engage all three channels for their revision – see it, hear it and do it, in whichever order that suits – it makes it easier for the learning to go in and easier for it to come back out again.

Physical movement in learning also actually helps us create connections between brain cells by causing us to release natural growth promoters called neurotrophins, especially 'brain-derived neurotrophic factor' or BDNF. This neurochemical has been referred to by Carl Cotman, a neuroscientist at the University of California, as 'brain fertilizer' such is its propensity for 'both prompting brain benefits on its own and triggering a cascade of other neural health-promoting chemicals to spring into action'. How much more gratifying this is than the abstract and unnatural 'sit and listen' or 'sit and read' strategies found in so many classrooms. Not only that, but the simple process of standing up actually increases the amount of oxygen coming into our brains by between 5 and 30 per cent depending on who you speak to (and remember how much oxygen our brains need). Just by standing up we can fire the brain with what it needs. Part of the chemical equation for creating the energy that our brains need is oxygen. Think of the lit candle when the jam jar goes over the top. Standing up and doing something with your hands higher than your heart improves the aerobic potential of the exercises, and then with one side of the body doing one thing and one doing another, you have a whole aerobic, energising cross-lateralisation exercise that wakes and shakes the whole brain.

'Misguided teachers who constantly tell their pupils to sit down and be quiet imply a preference for working with a group of trees, not a classroom full of people.'

Robert Sylwester, Professor Emeritus of Education at the University of Oregon, on how we sometimes can't see the wood for the children.

Energising your brain – some ideas for the classroom

Stand the students up and ask them to:

- Choose a keyword and write it in the air with one hand, then the other, then both at the same time.
- Choose a second keyword and write the first keyword with one hand and the second with the other.
- Draw from memory your Mindmap⋆ in the air.
- In pairs, write a name in the air that the other person has to copy and identify.
- With the front of the class being north, point to south–east, north–west …
- With the front of the class being 12.00, point to 6.30, 6.50 …
- Mime an experiment for a partner to guess.
- Point to where on the walls of the classroom/on the number washing line the answer to your question is … now do it with your eyes closed, now with both fingers.
- Arms stretched out either side, walk the 'line' and spell the new word at the same time.

Another strategy I have come across is that each time a child answers correctly he or she moves back one chair, the incentive being to end up as far from the teacher as possible.

Further evidence for ensuring a physical side to your lessons relates to a fascinating part of your brain, linked to the emotional brain, called the reticular activating system or RAS. Reticular comes from the Latin for 'a little net' and is the name given to a small but crucial network of neurons that deliver the wake-up call from deep in the brain to the neocortex, the message being 'wake up, something important is going on'. This is another reason why it is important to link what is taking place in your lessons to the goals and needs of the learners. With the RAS activated by focusing on the WIIFM? (see Chapter 1), the brain is more responsive to information coming in through all five senses. In other words, it is now on the alert for information and experiences that will help it achieve its goals. Indeed, the very process of having goals that we focus on regularly helps keep our RAS on the ball as it means the brain is primed to seek out and capture opportunities, experiences and knowledge that will help us achieve these goals. Without this important process taking place, we end up missing out on so much as the same opportunities, experiences and information simply pass us by. Ever heard that phrase, 'When my ship comes in, I'll be at the airport'?

So, how do the RAS and movement in the classroom tie together? Through the vestibular system – the part of our brains that helps us deal with balance, the awareness of our body in space and how to deal with the effects of gravity. By moving, we stimulate the vestibular system, by stimulating the vestibular system we alert the RAS, which in turns excites the neocortex to be on the alert for new information on its way in. So, the message is quite simple – especially when you realise that in boys the RAS takes more stimulation to get it going than in girls – stand up, if you want energised and motivated learners in your classroom who are open and alert to new information.

Putting it all together, we have the very real need for variety within variety in your lessons: for guaranteeing that each lesson you deliver has at least one opportunity to learn according to the learning preference of the student with all the many, many benefits – from more effective learning, to improvised memory, to better motivation – that such planning brings. And with variety comes a sense of control – a crucial key to motivation in the classroom.

In other words

- Ensure young people feel that they are in control.
- Offer opportunities for making choices.
- Encourage young people to take responsibility.
- Remember, you get control by giving it.
- Provide variety in the inputs of your lessons and encourage students to use variety in their revision.
- Refrain from imposing your preferred learning preferences on them.
- Use physical activities in your lessons.

Chapter 4

Get real

Sixteen years at 365 days a year or so makes around 5,840 days or 140,160 hours of life. Of that, starting school at 4½, being at school for seven hours a day, five days a week for forty weeks a year, I make it about 16,100 hours are spent in our lessons – or around 11.5 per cent of a young life. The actual research I have heard quoted puts the ratio at around 85:15 – perhaps they allow for training days. Either way, the amount of time children spend in school compared with outside school is a surprising statistic. And even that 15 per cent is in an environment that has been referred to by Chris Watkins in *Managing Classroom Behaviour from Research to Diagnosis* as 'the most complex and least understood situation on the face of the planet'.

Yet how often do we treat young people as if our time with them is the most important thing in the world? And if we are secondary teachers, we make our tiny proportion of the 15 per cent like that is the most important thing in the world.

It isn't.

> 'I found that it was only when I was using real numbers to solve real problems that maths made sense to me.'
>
> Richard Branson showing what it took to go from bottom of the class in maths to world-class businessman.

What are we doing, then, to bring the outside in and the inside out, to break down the barriers between the outside world and the hugely artificial environment that we call school? Ken Richardson quotes Raymond Meighan, a pioneer in the movement to alter what we mean by a school, as he puts into words the educational equivalent of what the little boy said about the sartorially challenged Emperor: ' ... it is the way children are subjected to artificial made-up subjects that are not embedded in cultural practice which renders most school learning tedious and irrelevant.'

> 'The hardest thing to explain is the glaringly evident which everybody had decided not to see.'
>
> Ayn Rand, writing in *The Fountainhead*, on why we need more little boys in the crowd telling it how it is.

Again, as with so much of the process of understanding how to get the best out of young people and help them motivate themselves for learning, we need to go back to the brain.

The 'wetware' between our ears (as opposed to hardware and software) is a parallel-processing unit with processing speeds almost impossible to comprehend – twenty million billion calculations per second, at around 250 miles an hour. We are designed to process many, many pieces of information simultaneously, thousands of which are coming into our brain through a variety of different sense-based inputs (subconsciously 100 million bits per second (bps) for our eyes, 30,000 bps for our ears, ten million bps through our sense of touch). Yet, to learn we feel that we need to slow things down, to chunk information into bite-sized pieces, to carve the world up into digestible morsels and, to extend the culinary metaphor to conceit, to separate the peas from the potatoes and the currants from the bun. These compartments which we call subjects at primary level, departments at secondary, and academic faculties beyond that, are a fallacious and arbitrary dissection of a far more complex and brain-friendly real world. Is maths that different from art at certain levels? Someone told me recently, if he had been told when he was at school what he knows now, that mathematics is an art, he would have enjoyed it a whole lot more. Is art totally separate from maths (the Golden Mean or 1:1.618 is found throughout nature and art)? Should food technology be taught by the science staff under the title 'molecular gastronomy'? What exactly *is* geography? And French, why, that's not even a subject at all! It's a medium, a means to an end. (In *sections bilingues* in some Canadian schools children learn French by using it to learn geography, for example.)

Ask a secondary teacher what they teach and the answer often comes back as 'French' or 'science' or 'Actually, I'm the head!' Ask a primary teacher and they look at you as if you have just asked them if they can spell their own name or tell you when the term ends. It is a non-question. The answer is simple: 'I teach children!' The gap between the teaching of children and the teaching of subjects is summed up in a line from a 1941 publication, entitled *The Future of Education*, by Sir Richard Livingstone, unearthed by John Abbott:

> The good schoolmaster is known by the number of valuable subjects he declines to teach.

Next time you meet someone who claims to be, for example, a science teacher, just look at them with incredulity and exclaim, 'You mean you don't teach young people about the beauty of art?' Go on, try it. You'll be a hit in the staffroom. (Although you may want to drop the indefinite article from that last sentence.) We expect children to become rounded individuals when they are taught by individuals who are not rounded (or at least not encouraged to show off their curved edges).

Our brain, then, is designed to process millions of pieces of information simultaneously, in a multisensory way, coming to it from a non-compartmentalised world. Learning in this way is not a problem. *Teaching* in this way, however, is where things start to get tricky. So, by splintering life into a variety of academic specialisms we again put the teaching ahead of the learning, impede the learning process by slowing it down and then blame the student if they switch off halfway through the course. Dog. Tail. Wagging. The. Please rearrange to form a sentence.

Another way of looking at this issue is through the bifocals of the left brain–right brain theory, something that recent research is showing to be more allegorical than accurate, but still useful when it comes to generating variety in our teaching. For decades we have been told that left-brain thinking includes areas such as language, logic, sequencing and working with component parts, whereas the right hemisphere has been associated with colours, shapes, rhythms, movement, emotion, intuition and what is known as the 'Big Picture'. While the reality is more complex than this, as is always the case with the human brain, it is worth taking another look at that list of so-called 'right-brain' thinking strategies. Does that describe the components of your average lesson? Do you teach predominantly to the 'left brain'? Thousands do. What about the 'right brain'? What about the 'whole brain' in our allegory? It's not a question of one set of strategies being better than the other; it's a question of using them all. Einstein would appear to have been a great 'whole-brain' thinker. Although he was a scientist and obviously had the sorts of skills associated with 'left-brain' thinking, he was also hugely creative, once being quoted as saying 'Imagination is more important than knowledge,' adding ' … for while knowledge points to all there is, imagination points to all there will be.' Many of his ideas came as a result of his *gedankenexperiments*, or thought experiments. If a man was falling through the universe in a lift and he shone a beam of light from a torch out through a hole in the side of the lift what would happen to that beam of light?

I have just come back from doing an INSET session with teachers in a special school in Wales, whose children were classed as having severe learning difficulties. They, in turn, had just come back from a four-day, Outward Bound-type experience at a camp with some of the older children, and one of the accompanying teachers was telling us the differences she had seen in her students. More energised, more creative, quicker to learn, more ready to use their own initiative – just some of the benefits she had found from just four days away. Despite the challenges thrown up by the wheelchairs and the learning difficulties, these children had responded to a new, challenging, immersive, multi-sensory, 'whole-brain' and real-life scenario in a way that had brought them – their learning and motivation – to life.

> 'Learning is experience. Everything else is just information.'
>
> Einstein on one of the differences between learning and teaching.

What are you doing in school, then, to take your children out of the artificial environment of the classroom? Have you ever seen your students outside of the four walls of your classroom? Have they ever seen you outside? Even from a simple memory point of view, this makes sense. One of the ways of looking at memory is to consider the difference between 'context' and 'content' memory. The latter is the memory associated with the classroom, with the 'here's a list of words, go away and learn them and I'll test you tomorrow' scenario, the difference between the textbook and the field trip, the learning of maths at the betting shop or dartboard versus the learning of the same principles in the classroom. 'Content' memory has been shown to be:

- very difficult to get into our heads; rote-learning works, but is hardly an inspiring strategy and there are others (do you need to rote-learn not to touch a hot saucepan?);
- difficult to change once it is in (if we learn it wrong, it tends to stay wrong);
- difficult to get out again (think of the students who let themselves down in the exam hall – they know it, it just doesn't come to them when they need it).

'Context' memory is the memory of the field trip or the trip to the zoo, of the athletics track or the French exchange. Apparently effortless, because you are focusing on a desired outcome other than the learning itself, it is a whole lot easier to get into your head, easier to manipulate and adapt once it is in there, and a great deal easier to get out again when you need it. Real life leads to real learning. As Rita Carter (in *Mapping the Mind*) says,

> Items of interest – those that ultimately have some bearing on survival – are retained better than those that are not. So personal and meaningful memories can be held in their brilliance while dry facts learned at school may soon fade away.

Think about that child in your class who may well remember nothing about the lessons he or she experienced yesterday but can remember every little detail about the school trip to the zoo three years ago. If it helps, think of our memories as one of our key tools for survival. We all have, I am convinced, brilliant memories. It's a question of learning how to use them. The brain wants to lay down memories for you, but only if it's important. How does it know if it's important? Apart from the sorts of things we have looked at earlier – emotions, movement, WIIFM?s and the RAS, to name but four – the brain receives a strong indicator of the need to have information close to hand if it is called on regularly. Take a look at the beginning of a graph (Figure 4.1). With time starting at the moment the lesson finishes, researchers have found that within ten minutes of the end of the learning period, our learning levels go up, something that has been called the 'reminiscence effect'. Our learning is clearer ten minutes after the lesson ends than immediately at the end. It is surmised that this happens as the brain exploits the 'quiet time' to take the new information and process it, put it away, as it were. Psychologists have a term they call 'in–out listening', that is, we can't be in two places at once. We are either 'outside' of

Time

Figure 4.1 The reminiscence effect

ourselves, listening to the wonderful words of wisdom from the teacher or 'inside' our heads making meaning of what we have just picked up, considering the implications for our own lives, reflecting on the learning. Sometimes, then, children are missing what we are teaching them as they are too busy trying to learn what we were just teaching them.

Something else at play here is the fact that we do not work at peak levels for long periods – the brain is not designed for that and instead works in cycles. Apart from our 12-hour, 24-hour and 29-day cycles, we also have cycles called ultradian rhythms, 90-minute cycles that take us through peak alertness to having a bit of a doze, and back again (for 90 minutes we breathe with our left nostril, our right brain more dominant, then we swap things around for the next hour and a half, before swapping back again). Even when we are asleep we still go through these 90-minute cycles of deep sleep followed by not-so-deep sleep. Dreaming, which happens as we pass through that hinterland between light sleep and deep sleep, also takes place in 90-minute cycles.

What this means in the classroom is that the idea of 'pulse-learning' may be more effective than trying to plough through an hour-long period, with the implication being if you miss anything, then there is either something wrong with you as a learner or me as a teacher. Pulse-learning implies cycling between activities of high challenge and low challenge, more stress–less stress, high focus–low focus as you go through your lessons. Fartlek, I hear you cry! Fartlek – speed play – is a Scandinavian form of training, best summed up by a teacher who described it as 'jog a lamppost, sprint a lamppost'. In other words, push yourself, then ease back, and then push again.

One of the things I am encouraging teachers to do as part of their lesson plans, or even lesson observations, is to look at their lessons as a timeline and then to describe the energy levels by way of an energy wave travelling across time. Does a traditional lesson of yours look like Figure 4.2 as your lesson matches the ebb and flow of the brains of your students? Over, say, a double period you may start with a high-energy warm-up activity to get them into the right state for learning (see information box), then bring them back down with some whole-class teaching perhaps, then bring them back up as they go about some physical task, back down again as they work in pairs to record what they have observed, then up again with some energisers to reinforce the learning, down once again to write up what they have learned, and then end with some high-energy activity to send them out feeling good. (For shorter lessons, apply the same principle, but simply oscillate less!)

Energy

Time

Figure 4.2 Fartlek in the classroom.

Mental limbering up

Think of the brain like a muscle. For example, we have seen in Chapter 2 that we can grow our brains, but bear in mind they should also be limbered up, like muscles, before use. In the same way that we wouldn't expect a sprinter to race without warming up first, it is the same thing for the brain. Research has shown that mental limbering up makes for more effective learning. How do you limber up the brains of your students at the start of the lesson? I always start my INSET sessions with a creative-thinking exercise which means that, because there are no rights or wrongs, everyone has the chance to start thinking without the added unnecessary stress of worrying about being right or wrong. In other words, it has all the benefits of mental limbering up for learning without the downside of failure, as you can't be wrong because it's just a piece of nonsense.

'I like nonsense, it wakes up my brain cells.'

Dr Seuss on how, when it comes to the use of nonsense for learning, the cat in the hat is out of the bag.

Some teachers use Dingbats or anagrams, or write, for example, the word 'glaciation' on the board and see how many words of three letters or more the students can make out of it, whoever finds the most being allowed to choose and write up the word for the next lesson. It is a very useful strategy, especially with certain boys, I am told, as it reduces the amount of time they have from walking into a lesson, sitting down, waiting for the lesson to start, and thinking to themselves, 'How shall I fill the time creatively?' Another school that I had worked with now uses such a strategy throughout every department. The teachers reported to me that apart from being a useful buffer to help cope with students turning up late for lessons – the rest of the class is on-task, but you don't have to backtrack for the latecomers as they beat away the smell of cigarettes – many of the students who used to be late for lessons are now first in the queue because they want to know what the question, the challenge, the lateral-thinking exercise is for today.

Does that describe the lesson you gave last Thursday afternoon, for example? One primary school I worked with had taken the need for bringing the children's energy levels up to such an extent that their lessons looked more like Figure 4.3. I had to interject on more than one occasion and have the children lying on the floor listening to classical music with their eyes closed as they quietly reviewed what they had been learning. That said, many teachers admit to energy waves in their classes that are more akin to Figure 4.4. This is where everyone starts low and then gets lower ('In the first peak little Danny lost his pencil. In the second we had a wasp come in, but by the end of the lesson we were all unconscious … ').

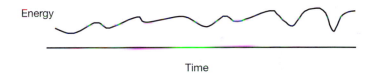

Figure 4.3 The over-energised classroom.

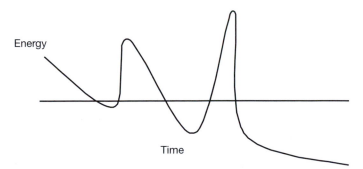

Figure 4.4 Flatliners!

Anyway, back to the ten minutes just after the lesson ended (Figure 4.1). Twenty-four hours later the learning levels have moved on – or should I say down. According to the research of a Herr Ebbinghaus (backed up by the testimony of anyone who has ever sat in a classroom), within 24 hours up to 80 per cent of the information has disappeared (Figure 4.5). The Ebbinghaus Curve of Forgetting is not a novel by Milan Kundera but a very real process going on in our classrooms which renders so much of our teaching a complete waste of time. For every 100 minutes that we work, eighty of them are wasted. Every year 11 student who sits at his or her desk to revise for an hour and then stands up and walks away has left behind them 80 per cent of what they had just learned. Unless, that is, we go into our brains again and look at what is going on as they take new information on board.

At a simple level, when we learn new things, brain cell A has spoken to brain cell B for the first time. For up to about a day or so afterwards, these newly acquainted brain cells are chemically and electrically active, alert, ready to fire again. If we don't fire them again within that window, the state of readiness

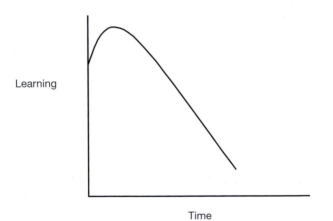

Figure 4.5 The Ebbinghaus Curve of Forgetting.

fades away, as if it was never there in the first place. Rita Carter describes the way the memory seems to disappear as being like the 'buttocks–shaped hollow in a foam rubber cushion as you stand up'.

> 'Patterns that produce thoughts (and thus behaviours) that help the organism to thrive are laid down permanently while those that are useless fade. '

> Rita Carter on why we sometimes forget how to ask the way to the ironmongers in French.

How much of our teaching is nothing more than a 'buttocks-shaped hollow in a foam rubber cushion'? We teach, the children try and learn, they forget, we get frustrated, they get despondent, everyone's motivation suffers. Yet we do know how to address this problem simply. You *review*.

This is the ideal review cycle according to the research:

- You review again at the end of the lesson (some secondary schools have even been so bold as to start reviewing the previous lesson's material in the next lesson to make the most of the reminiscence effect, reviewing the French lesson you have just come from at the beginning of the maths lesson you have just walked into. What I also like about this is that it starts to hack away, brick by brick, at the walls that have been artificially constructed between subject areas).
- You review again within 24 hours. Please note that this is best done using open-type questioning – 'You have one minute: in pairs, identify the three most important things you remember from yesterday's lesson' – as opposed to closed-type questions – 'Hands up who can remember the French for cabbage'. In the latter, not everyone will become engaged and subsequently will fail before they have even started, and even those who can remember will only be re-firing a fraction of the memories they have. In the former, everyone can remember something, no one fails,

everyone participates, there are no rights or wrongs and a great deal of the memories can be re-fired.

- Review again after a week – four or five minutes is all that is needed, it will be there. You will be amazed. So will they.
- Review again after a month – three or four minutes, now, that's all.
- And then review again after six months.

Adopting this cycle has been shown to increase the efficacy of our memories by as much as 400 per cent! And make sure you tell your children about this process, too, so they can do it independently of you. Encourage them to ask themselves, as they walk out of the lesson, 'What are the three most important things I have learned today?' And as they head home at the end of the day, 'What are the three most important things I have learned in each lesson I have had today?'

I know of one primary teacher who now has her children rehearse in pairs at the end of the day three answers to the question beloved of so many parents, 'What did you learn at school today, dear?' (Although the query, 'What questions did you ask at school today, dear?' was apparently the preferred style of Mrs Einstein to the young Albert.) Make sure that the students who are revising close their books at the end of the period of revision, pull out a blank sheet of paper and review everything they have just been learning (Mindmaps★ are good for this), and then walk away. The following day, as they start their revision, again, on a blank sheet of paper, 'What was I doing yesterday?', then start today's revision. Building a review timetable into the revision timetable is a useful way of making sure this is done.

This process of review is the process that we naturally use in order to develop habits – and it has been suggested that over 90 per cent of our life is habit. If we start to develop better habits, then, we will make some real changes all round. Mindmaps★, for example, can seem most unnatural to begin with, but over time using them will become a habit. However, the more you do something the stronger the connections, the more 'habitual' it will become as you move into 'unconscious competence' mode, the realm of the habit. Sooner, rather than later, the principles involved in a book such as this one start to become habits, and you are not even aware of what you are doing, but it just seems to have worked.

> 'We are what we repeatedly do. Excellence, then, is not an act but a habit.'

> Aristotle on how the only practice that makes perfect is perfect practice.

In the 'real world' review like this will take place naturally as we learn the skills and knowledge we need in order to survive. We are, after all, natural learners. Even your so-called least able child has learned – and is continuing to learn – a great deal. I once asked James Dyson, of dual cyclone fame, what his advice would be to two very different sorts of school leaver – one with all the qualifications you could wish for, the other with nothing. To the first, he said, his recommendation would be that he or she had shown that they had a brain and that they should now go out and use it. To the second he would say, 'It doesn't matter.' Dyson was definitely not saying that qualifications are not important; indeed, he prefers employing graduates straight out of college (before they become sullied by the cynical world of work). However, he was underlining the reality of the situation – that you still have a great deal to offer, no matter what you leave school with, that it is never too late, and that this is never 'as good as it gets' unless we accept it like that. In other words, perhaps we should be brave enough to say to some of our less high-achieving students, 'School? It's just a phase you are going through!'

> 'Most of the world's leaders found school to be an uncomfortable, if not disastrous, experience.'

> Howard Gardner on *Leading Minds* and how they are not necessarily the greatest minds.

A business magazine I once read had an article in it about successful entrepreneurs, entitled 'Unqualified success', in which six entrepreneurs were profiled. (They were all male, although as I point out to the girls in my events, in 1997 of all new business start-ups, that's around 150,000 businesses, 30 per cent were started by women.) Between them, at that time, they were worth £678 million. Between them they had three O-levels. In the article Chris Lewis, author of *The Unemployables*, suggested that:

> To succeed in business you need determination, creativity, self belief, bravery, positivity and sheer energy.

Can you think of young people you are working with who perhaps enjoy little success at school but who have the above qualities by the bucket-load? Without in any way condoning joyriding, I would suggest that you need to have most of those attributes to do it. What are the opportunities for *encouraging*, *developing* and *celebrating* such characteristics in your lessons – and for all students? After all, I have come across many who were doing very well at school yet showed very few of such crucial attributes.

> 'I was never given a mark for creativity at school, I was told don't be different. But only "dead fish go with the river".'
>
> James Dyson, on how success can come from not doing what you are told at school.

One of the exercises I ask young people to do is to give themselves a score out of ten for each of the six attributes Lewis described above, and then add them up together for an 'employ-ability score'. I remind them then that they have a responsibility to make sure they are raising their own score – on a weekly basis, if not daily. If they scored four out of ten for bravery, what are they going to do by the end of the week to be hitting five out of ten, at least? Little steps towards big goals.

How to be the first to fly solo across the Atlantic

In the race to be the first to fly solo across the Atlantic in the first half of the last century, Charles Lindbergh showed he would do whatever he had to do in order to succeed and, at the same time, showed how malleable our personalities are if we have the desire — the WIIFM? or the *ganas* — to change. In his book, *Charles Lindbergh – An Autobiography*, Leonard Mosley quotes Lindbergh as he drew up a list of rules to live by:

> I came to the conclusion that if I knew the difference between the right way to do something and the wrong way to do it, it was up to me to train myself to do the right thing at all times. So I drew up a list of character factors.

Lindbergh identified sixty-five factors, including 'alertness, altruism, ambition, aptitude, balance, brevity, concentration, diligence, enterprise, foresight, honesty, intuition, judiciousness, manliness, orderliness, precision, quiet temperedness, reserve, solicitude, tact, usefulness, watchfulness, zeal … ' which he then used to mould his personality in order to achieve his goal. As Mosley points out, 'He then changed from a quiet, taciturn, serious, solitary man to a convivial, hand-shaking one … but only if it brought him nearer to the attainment of his objective.'

This process of little steps towards big goals is something that actor and singer Will Smith learned in a very powerful manner from his father as he was growing up in America. In a loving and caring way his dad made the 12-year-old Smith and his brother build a brick wall that was 50 feet long and 14 feet high. After six months of hard work, and upon completion of the task, his father had these words for him: 'Now don't tell me there is anything you can't do.' It is a lesson for us all – if there's any DIY to do, trick your children into doing it for you. 'Hey kids, who wants to play shed building?' For Smith the message was loud and clear:

> There's nothing insurmountable if you keep laying bricks … You go on one at a time and eventually there will be a wall … I just concentrate on the bricks and the walls take care of themselves.

In Chapter 1 we saw how, as far as coach John Wooden was concerned, success was being better than you were yesterday. It also makes sense to have a working definition of failure to serve us well in the world outside of school, one that can move us beyond the artificial yes/no, right/wrong, black/white world of the classroom. One of the most useful interpretations of failure I can possibly imagine is the simple understanding that it does not even exist. Call it 'feedback' or 'learning' but never failure. After all, failure is no more than an intellectual concept. It's just the non-achievement of what we set out to achieve in the first place, yet you can't achieve nothing, nature abhorring a vacuum. If I set out to achieve A grades and 'fail', I haven't simply ended up with nothing. I have 'B' grades, or whatever it may be. More importantly, I have learned how *not* to get A grades and how to get B grades. Like so much, it's a matter of perspective or, in psychological terms, a process of re-framing.

> 'I've made more mistakes in the 18 years I've been doing this job than probably any human being in America.'
>
> Former GE CEO Jack Welch, overlooking George W. Bush's prowess as a public speaker.

Now, I know it's not as easy as that at an emotional level, and the feelings associated with not achieving what we set out to achieve are very powerful ones indeed – I should know. One of the worst days of my working life came as a result of my dream of a big event to help schools grab the opportunities of life at the turn of the century, an all-singing, all-dancing event. It was a disaster and it took a lot out of me. Yet I know how much I have learned from it. I also know that at least I tried.

The idea of learning through 'failure' is fundamental to our own development. We fall over many times before we learn to walk. We talk rubbish for many years before we get elected. We learn more from 'failure' than we do from the philosophy of 'right first time'. If you only read one business book in your life, read *Funky Business* by Kjell Nordström and Jonas Ridderstråle and do it, if not for your sake, for the sake of your students, who will be entering the world that these two business PhDs describe so brilliantly, even if you're not. In it they suggest that we have to 'fail faster to learn quicker to succeed sooner' and quote Albert Yu, senior vice-president at silicon chip-makers Intel, who argued that, 'Failure is just part of the culture of innovation. Accept it and become stronger.'

Remember the farcical attempt by Coca-Cola to introduce a new recipe in the 1980s? The whole exercise cost millions of dollars yet the man behind the 'failure', Sergio Zyman, Coca-Cola's chief global marketeer, was soon back at the corporation. Although it was aborted after just 79 days, the 'New Coke' debacle led to the biggest ever one-year rise in sales, reversing a sharp decline. As Zyman said, 'We get paid to produce results. We don't get paid to be right.'

> '**We become uncompetitive by not being tolerant of mistakes. The moment you let avoiding failure become your motivator you're down the path of inactivity. You can stumble only if you're moving.'**
>
> **Former CEO Robert Goizueta, showing how Coca-Cola would like to teach the world to screw up.**

Ask any child – as I frequently do – to name a successful person and the name Richard Branson usually comes up. Yet it is important that young people learn that his undoubted success is built on the back of many, many failures. These range from a Christmas tree business he started when he was still at school (rabbits ate the stock), and a budgerigar breeding business he started soon afterwards (they bred so well he saturated the market and his mother let them all go) to the millions he spent launching a competitor to the London listings magazine *Time Out*, called *Event,* that flopped. This is not to mention his 'failure' to cross the Atlantic in a speedboat the first time (picked out of the sea by the coastguard off Ireland), his 'failure' to fly his hot air balloon across the Pacific the first time (they inflated it, it fell apart) and his on-going 'failure' to fly around the world in yet another doomed hot air balloon.

> **'An almost unlimited capacity to swallow failure and humiliation.'**
>
> **Would children recognise this view of Richard Branson as described in his biography *Virgin King*: by Tim Jackson?**

Success and what we call failure go hand in hand. As Woody Allen once said, 'If you're not failing every now and again it's a sign that you are not doing anything very innovative.' If this is the case, and bearing in mind the role we play as role models to our students, to what extent are you role modelling this notion in your classroom? Do you have an environment and ethos in your school in which it is OK to share with your colleagues your experiences of the things that did not work out as you had planned? Can you sit down with a heavy groan in the staffroom at lunchtime, head in hands, and explain to your concerned colleagues how your fully interactive multimedia lesson on the building of the Great Pyramids for 4C descended into the sorts of scenes the class hamster will take a long time to recover from? Would you be met with professional support and congratulations for what you attempted and with suggestions as to how you could have prevented the bloodshed? Or will the old lag sniff into his copy of the *Guardian* and suggest that *he* never has any trouble with them so it must be something *you* are doing wrong?

If you are on the management team of your school, how do you react to the mistakes of your staff? More importantly, how do your staff think you will react? I am convinced that there is more unadventurous teaching because of the mindset which asks 'what will the Head say if she sees me doing this?' than as a result of a fear of Ofsted or of what the children may do. Do you actively encourage your staff not only to experience 'failure' but also to share it afterwards? Do you expect them to 'fail' from time to time and begin to ask uncomfortable questions of them if they have no 'cock-ups' to share?

> 'Mistakes will be made but if a person is essentially right, the mistake he or she makes are not as serious as the mistakes the management will make if it is dictatorial and undertakes to tell those under its authority exactly how they must do their jobs.'

> Dr William E. Coyne, 3M's senior vice-president, R&D, on how pyramids can go pear-shaped. It was by following their own advice that 3M created a glue that didn't stick and made a packet out of Post-it® pads.

And what about what happens within the four walls of your classroom itself? Do you have the sort of relationship with your students whereby you can stand in front of them and explain that you are about to do something you've never tried before, so you don't know if it will work, but you're going to have a go anyway and see what happens, and then afterwards you'll all discuss how it was and how it could be even better next time?

> 'I would rather be accused of being over-ambitious than of being lily-livered.'

> Architect Sir Norman Foster, quoting – and ignoring – Macbeth simultaneously.

Most students have the opportunity to learn and practise strategies for coping with failure during the course of their school careers. However, there is a particular group who may leave school without ever having fully developed these life – and life-saving – skills and for whom the whole concept of failure is something strange and foreign to contemplate. We call these poor children 'more able' students. One of the big messages coming through from the specialists in the whole area of stretching the gifted and talented high-achieving students in our schools, people such as David George, is that we are doing young people a disservice by not making sure they fail from time to time during their school careers.

One of the most famous definitions of intelligence comes from the granddaddy of child development theory, Jean Piaget, who declared that:

> Intelligence is what you use when you don't know what to do.

Yet we spend our teaching lives setting up situations in which we explain in great detail exactly what we want our students to do and help them to do it bit by bit in what you may call a 'prepare-then-do' model. One headteacher I once spoke to said that it was a bit like giving them a crossword that we have already filled in for them and asking them to go over the words (did someone say wordsearch?) in neat writing.

'Me havin' no education, I had to use my brains.'

Liverpool FC's legendary Bill Shankley, demonstrating Piaget's definition of intelligence in a way that footballers can understand.

Piaget, then, is suggesting that we make sure that students also have the opportunity to explore a 'do-then-prepare' model. Throw them in at the deep end and see who swims. Not recommended, I know, if you are a PE teacher but essential elsewhere. So, hidden between the accolades and school prizes, the merit certificates and UCAS forms lies a gremlin that may undermine the success beyond school of some of your most successful students – the inability to know what to do when they don't know what to do. Research in learning science backs up the duty we, as teachers, have to make sure we confuse and confound all our students from time to time. Known by various names from the straightforward 'managed confusion' to (my favourite) 'orchestrated disequilibrium', the principle is that an element of confusion actually makes for a far more effective learning transaction.

> 'CASE teachers are trained to maximise cognitive confusion.'
>
> Dr Carol McGuiness of Queen's University, Belfast, in her governmental report on the need to focus 'not only on what is to be learned but on how children learn' and how confusion helps accelerate the learning of effective thinking.

It seems to work on the idea of what psychologists call 'cognitive dissonance', the brain not liking to be out of balance and always doing what it can to get back to balance and wholeness again. This search for completeness underlies *Gestalt* theory and has been responsible for many a 'two plus two equals five' misunderstanding. Because of the brain's dislike for this imbalance, deliberately creating such a scenario in the classroom will act to motivate the student to seek out the answers in an active manner to make the situation whole again. Done in a managed and supportive way, confusion is your friend in the classroom, yet how many of us have been criticised in teaching when the observer – from your teacher training tutor to an inspector – points out that at one point the students were 'a bit confused'.

In a class of year 10 students I once taught there was a very bright young lad who went on to achieve top grades in his GCSEs and A-levels and no doubt beyond. During one lesson I had asked the students to copy a table from the board into their exercise books. The boy in question called me over and asked me how, exactly, I wanted the table copied into his book – sideways, lengthways, across two pages? I simply told him he could do it how he saw fit, at which point he became very irate and blurted, 'Tell me what to do and I'll do it!' A very bright lad but one from whom all sense of self-determination seemed to have been taken to be replaced with an 'I need to play by the rules, so I need to know the rules' mentality. (A mentality which, by the way, is probably serving him very well indeed in his chosen career, as his ambition was to go and join the armed forces.)

One student teacher I heard about simply put up the words 'El Niño' on the board and let the class get on with working out what it was all about. The whole department was very impressed with the work that came out as a result of the exercise. So, *clarity with vagueness* I now find is the best way to set tasks for students (including the teachers I work with). No matter how precise I used to think I had made the instructions, there was always one student who would come up with a whole new interpretation of how to perform the task, not the way I had intended but often very valuable in its own right. These days I set a task that is *specific* in terms of focus but can be vague in terms of process. This limits the unnecessary time and effort I had to put in to issuing supposedly exacting instructions and reduces the opportunity for conflict when the student – often a boy, girls always seem more keen to please than to catch out – would manage to do the task in a way that involved not doing the task.

Offering opportunities for students to think for themselves takes time if they are not used to it but really does start to prepare them for success beyond a mere academic existence. There are a number of secondary schools that have made a start in this process of opening up school learning beyond academic success, yet there is still a certain stigma attached to the area of 'work-related learning'. You need to address this consciously if such programmes are going to succeed. One girls' school changed the bland and socially unacceptable name of the work-related learning programme to the rather more ambitious 'How to be a Healthy and Successful 21st Century Woman'. The programme coordinator is now fighting off girls who previously wouldn't have wanted anything to do with the course. (Ah, the power of advertising.)

In many ways, a great deal of what we are talking about here boils down to attitude – something that will take you further faster than your qualifications. In the words of an ad. I saw on the London Underground for the employment agency Brook Street: 'We're all temps now … Forget the Euro. Attitude is the new currency.'

> 'In business an attitude shortage is at least as bad as a skills shortage … members said motivation, commitment to high quality work and a desire to learn were more important than communication, numeracy and team working.'
>
> Former director-general of the CBI, Adair Turner, in an address to the NUT in 1997 on the need for *ganas* at work and how, before you can count what you make, you need to make yourself count. Subsequent research by the CBI identified that only 9 per cent of members said qualifications were the most important thing to look for in employees.

When working with young people one of the first things I do is to ask them to raise their hands if they want to be successful. They nearly always all do. Now I have them where I want them, I can then help them understand that the achievement of the success they say they want depends on their answer to three questions.

1 What do you want?

Bearing in mind we can't go shopping for something that we don't know exists we need an answer to this question. Another way of looking at it is to give the students the example of what they are given for their birthday if they aren't specific about what they want. (The answer here they usually shout is 'socks', although one lad once shouted, 'A dress!' which was surprising enough until he added, 'but not the one I wanted.') In other words, if you don't know what you want, how are you going to get it? For more information on how such a question ties in with goal-setting, along with the questions to help them come up with answers, see Chapter 1.

> 'It's not because I make money that I am realising my dream: first of all it's because I am doing what I want to do.'
>
> Ralph Lauren, a glove salesman with no drawing ability who became the head of his own fashion house.

2   How much do you want it?

A handy way of asking students to respond to a question such as 'how much do you want to be successful?' is to give it a score out of ten, with ten being top. Once they have identified a number I tell them the story of Socrates taking down to the shores of the sea a student who had asked him how he could be as wise as the great teacher. Socrates took the student into the sea and then forcibly held his head under water until the student finally managed to break free and come up gasping for air. 'When you were under the water what did you want?' asked Socrates. 'Air, I had to have air!' came the reply from the bedraggled student, making a mental note not to ask questions in class any more. 'That,' retorted Socrates triumphantly, 'is what it takes when it comes to wanting wisdom!' If you want success, you can have it, but how much do you really want it?

> 'You are what your deep driving desire is.'
>
> Sanskrit words of wisdom from the Upanishads. So what does that make us if we have no deep, driving desire?

3   What are you going to do about it?

It's easy to say what you want and how much you want it but actually getting off your backside and doing it can be more problematic for many people. Yet, here again is an example of how life's high achievers are differentiated from the others in the world beyond school. As the line goes, 'For every hundred people who stand around explaining why something can't be done there is always someone getting up and doing it.' For example, many young boys think the key to success at football is simply skill and luck. (As a great golfer once said – although which one depends on what source you look at – 'The more I practise, the luckier I become!') What many miss is the effort put into being skilful. There really is no such thing as an overnight success. Above Alex Ferguson's desk at Old Trafford is the Latin phrase, taken from the gates of Govan Shipyard, '*Non sine labore*' – not without effort. Put it above your desk too. Whenever students express a goal, it is important to ask them what specifically they did yesterday to move them closer to their goal. If the answer was they did nothing, then they are not so much standing still as moving away from their goal. Like the heat-seeking missile, if it is not moving closer to its target, it is moving further away. What, *specifically*, do they have planned today to move them towards their goal? And tomorrow?

> 'It's not the beginning but the continuing of the game until it be thoroughly finished that yieldeth the true glory.'
>
> Sir Francis Drake with the philosophy behind that game of bowls in a letter to Sir Francis Walsingham.

My message to young people: make sure you are making the most of education (I ask them to write the word 'learning' and then put a finger over the first letter to help them remember why), and ensure too that you are doing it in a way that combines academic success with a great attitude. With both together there will be no stopping you. What else, then, can you do in and outside of your classroom to help them achieve this?

In other words

- Remember how small a part of young people's lives your subject is.
- Look for links between the inside and the outside.
- Review regularly.
- Plan for an effective 'energy wave'.
- Encourage confusion.
- Model a 'failure as feedback' approach to life.
- Actively focus on the 'success attitude' in your classroom.

Chapter 5

Get personal

The one thing I learned from my teacher training is that teaching is about relationships. Once you get those right, children will leap through hoops of flame for you. Get them wrong – and it can feel like the other way round.

Let me take you back to a defining difference that I have observed between the primary sector and the secondary sector. In the former, teachers teach children. In the latter, teachers teach subjects. However, expecting children to be motivated to learn your subject because: (a) you are, and (b) they have to, is not enough. Human behaviour will out, and if I am going to spend time with you doing what you ask of me, then I need some sort of relationship with you for it to work.

I know that in a busy schedule asking children about how they got on in the athletics, or whether they saw the match last night, or if they enjoyed their holiday can be pushed to one side quite easily. Building relationships, however, is an *investment* of your time and energy that pays back many times and in many ways. My son had, in many ways, what can be described as a lousy relationship with one of his classroom teachers for a time when he was at primary school. Things just did not seem to click between them. Yet part-way through the year they went on a week-long field trip to the east coast (not just the two of them, the whole class went, we thought it best). By the end of that week, bridges had been built, understandings had been come to, relationships had been developed. It takes time and it takes energy and it's worth it.

WIIFM?s, relationships and the internal motivation
A head of year once told me how he had been working
with a girl who had been ejected from a lesson because of
her behaviour. Trying to encourage her to go back to the
lesson to work, he tried a number of potential WIIFFM?s,
all to no avail. Finally, out of desperation he said, 'Will
you do it for me?' to which she replied, 'OK then,' and
happily went back to work. Is this an example of internal
or external motivation? Because the relationship between
student and adult was so good, I think she was motivated
from within to please him.

What are the opportunities for engaging with your students
in a setting beyond the four walls of your classroom? It could
be from the trip abroad to the field trip to the community
work with the old people down the road – something that lets
everyone see each other in a different light and wearing different
masks.

A great friend and colleague of mine is a man called Jim
Roberson, the self-styled Discipline Coach and a larger than
life Black American from New York and a former professional
American football player. He is currently living and working in
a challenging community on the south coast of England doing
all sorts of amazing things with young people, whose view of
life and the opportunities they have in that life could otherwise
be very limited. One of the things he has been doing with these
youngsters, for several years now, is running a trip to New York
in the early spring. He has negotiated various deals and calls on
various favours (his dad drives the group around in a big, yellow
school bus when they get there) and manages to take a large
party each year. Now, bear in mind that some of these children
have never been to the other side of their home town, let alone
walked around Central Park. And they are children who very
often have either been rejected by or have themselves rejected
the school system. But in the words of the big man himself:

How do we change if we've never experienced anything else?

Another scheme he set up was a 'work appreciation programme', based on his own experience growing up in the US. Here young people not only had work placements during the summer but were also paid for what they did, with money going into a special bank account that Jim had set up for them after negotiations with one of the large banks. If there was money in their account a few months later, the bank even gave them a little extra to reward their ability to save. With different experiences and new responsibilities what happened was that many of these young people managed to stay on through the school system – the building of relationships and the new opportunities serving to bring out the best in them in the classroom.

But you don't have to take 9B to the other side of the world in order to build motivating relationships. You can do it in your classroom and for free. How? By using a technique that I know from my experience of walking down school corridors (especially secondary ones) and sitting in lessons (both secondary *and* primary) and one that many teachers, shall we say, 'forget' to use, despite the fact that it costs nothing, takes no time to prepare or deliver and makes *them* feel good at the same time. The technical term we use is – smiling.

What is the first thing that your students see as they come into your classroom, for example? Is it your smiling face welcoming them in? For some of you, of course it is; the question is hardly worth asking. We call those teachers 'primary teachers'. For others, however, this may not be the case. A teacher from a school in the north-east of England told me once how, because the school was beginning to experience certain problems with discipline and behaviour, all staff had been instructed to stand at their doors as the children were entering the classrooms and 'look fierce'. When it became clear that this was not doing the trick and behaviour was still deteriorating, the edict went out that staff were also to stand at their doors and look fierce as the students were on the way out at the end of the lesson. I kid you not. The teacher who was giving me this inside information (on, I must say, what is perceived to be a 'good' school) told me that once she had been walking down the corridor and happily wished a cheery 'Good morning' to one of her colleagues outside his classroom to which the man replied, with his hand held up to halt her attempt at pleasantries, 'Don't interrupt me, I'm controlling the class. They're a new group and I need to concentrate.'

> 'If the head goes in with a long face – or an impartial face – teaching and learning will be negatively affected for the day.'
>
> Professor Tim Brighouse on how the quality of the head depends on the face.

A baby's eyes come into focus at around 13 inches, roughly the distance between baby and mother during breast-feeding. One of the very first images we focus on is the smiling (if not a little tired) face of our mother. That image of two eyes and smiley face stays with us, deep down in our psyche. When someone smiles at us, an automatic smile response is triggered whether we like it or not. Something fires that distant memory and we smile back, we start to feel good whether we like it – or even notice it – or not. I am aware that there are some teachers who have managed to suppress their automatic smile response through years of abuse and dubious INSET. Even so, research has found that the muscles around our mouth do react, albeit imperceptibly, when someone smiles at us. In other words, you can turn a class around with a smile.

A teacher once complained to me about her 'least favourite' class so I suggested she should treat them *as if they were her favourite class*. Despite her misgivings she gave it a go. Within four weeks, she later told me, she had turned that class round. How did she do it? She welcomed them in. She looked pleased to see them. She said thank you for coming. She gave off the message, 'I enjoy teaching you, challenging though you are. Come again soon won't you!' Now, I may be paraphrasing a little there but the message is certainly an important one. Do you ever stand in front of a class and give off the message – if not consciously, at least unconsciously – 'I don't want to be here and I don't want you to be here either'? Yet you have a moral, ethical and professional responsibility not to be putting across such a message. After all, of all the people in the room, you are the only one who could walk away and never come back and you wouldn't be arrested. The students have to be there and they are not even being paid.

One teacher who put such a simple strategy into operation was a male teacher from a secondary school in the south of England. He used to be one of many, many teachers who made it a professional point of honour to look stern and preoccupied in the corridors. However, he then started to smile at his students as he walked through the school, even strike up the odd conversation ('Did you see the football last night?' as opposed to the more traditional and commonplace, 'Tuck that shirt in, Jones!'). These days, he told me, he is often found in the corridors with a small group of lads around him chatting about real-life things, with the benefits of improved relationships – and work – in the classroom with those boys.

Another benefit of being able to smile 'at will', as it were, is the fact that the students don't get to see when they might be getting to you. If we say that a certain amount of student behaviour from certain quarters is designed to 'wind up' the teacher, then the ability to hang on to your smile come what may means that you will always thwart this effort so that the perpetrators may then move on to other activities in the classroom. My very first teaching job involved working with a 'bottom-set' group of students who prided themselves on the number of teachers they had driven to reaching for the Prozac. I made it my mission with these children *not* to shout and to remain calm and smiling no matter what they did. They soon became very frustrated indeed, asking me why I didn't shout, obviously confused that I wasn't playing the game. No matter what happened I was always in control of myself (with all the positive implications that brings – see Chapter 3), even though I wasn't necessarily in control of them at first (although fortunately they didn't know that).

Shouting as a result of a short fuse or lack of self-control will undermine you faster than you can say 'Who do you think you are?' I have heard so much unnecessary bellowing in schools that is of benefit to no one, let alone the teacher making all the noise. As I wrote in my notebook during a teaching practice some years ago,

Why do teachers shout at students? Because they can!

A useful little strategy for grabbing the attention of a class without raising your voice, and which is probably as old as the hills – although I was not taught it during my teacher training – is to stand at the front and raise your arm with a confident yet expectant look on your face. The first time I tried this in a classroom (I had recently seen it work in a room full of about 2,500 people as a demonstration of the power of non-verbal communication) within a minute I was surprised to find that I had a whole classroom sitting there with their hands up and an expectant look on their faces. So, while we were at it, we raised the other hand and then went down to the right, down to the left, clapped our hands three times and began the lesson!

Achieving what you want without resorting to asking for what you want is a useful strategy in its own right in any classroom and, again, is a sign that you are building rapport with your students. Another similar strategy is the 'hot spot' idea. Rather than having to raise your voice to, for example, ask a class to be quiet and in doing so actually force them to talk more loudly as they raise their voices to get over the noise of your shouting, you quieten them down by simply changing where you stand. Your teaching 'space' – usually towards the front of the class, near your table or bench and the whiteboard – is a position they have learned subconsciously to associate with you teaching whilst they learn. Just by seeing you there they are expecting to learn. And if you deliver what you do with a smile on your face, then they know that while you are there all will be well. However, to tell them off always go to a different part of your room, an area that you would never normally go to for any other reason.

This is your 'discipline hot spot'. It doesn't take long before they realise that whenever you are standing in your teaching 'hot spot' everything is fine. But when they find you in your discipline one they know something's up. In fact, it doesn't take long before all you need to do is to walk in the direction of the 'hot spot' and they start to feel something's wrong, even at a subconscious level, and the noise starts to go down without, often, any of the students knowing what has happened. What you are also doing here is talking to them in a language which, especially for the students with a 'kinaesthetic preference' (*ergo* some of the boys), is the language they work with best – non-verbal language.

I have seen so many assemblies at which the head of year, for example, will be standing at the front of the hall as the students are coming in and then have trouble trying to start his or her assembly *from the same spot*. Always supervise the entry to assembly from the sides and then move to the front when you want to start the ball rolling. It's amazing how powerful this is.

Motorvation

One of the benefits of smiling is the effect that it has on the smiler as well as on the smiled at. When we smile the very process of smiling causes us to release happy chemicals – endorphins – that make us feel good. In other words, we don't have to wait to feel good to smile. Smiling can make us feel good. This works because we are what is known as 'psycho-dynamic beings' – our physiology can have an effect on our psychology.

If we want to be motivated – and remember that the word 'motivation' comes from the Latin 'to move' – then we can achieve this by acting motivated. If that sounds far-fetched, then bear in mind what the All Blacks rugby team get up to just before a match. The Haka war dance is a breathtaking example of psycho-dynamics in action. The players use their bodies and voices to ready their brains for action (and in psyching themselves up, they psyche the opposition out).

Consider colleagues you meet who are always telling people who will listen how depressed they are (they are not really depressed, otherwise they wouldn't be telling other people). Apparently, one of the best ways to deal with them is simply to go up to them and, with an interested look on your face, ask, 'Wow, how do you do that?' The answer, if you observe closely, is usually to wear a lot of black, look down a lot, speak in a brow-beaten way and listen to a lot of Leonard Cohen.

We have access to whatever state we want, when we want it, simply by acting as if we were already in that state. If you want to be motivated, act motivated. To be happy, act happy. To be confident, act confident. By changing your physiology you change your psychology.

One thing I have noticed, especially among girls, is a particular way of standing when they are asked to give a talk to a class or an assembly. It is a stance I call the 'one-legged elephant' position, whereby they stand legs crossed, one hand across the body holding the other arm, with the head – and quite often most of the body – tilted to one side. Not a confidence-giving way to stand. Teaching young people how to look confident (feet slightly apart, grounded, eyes front, back straight, smile on your face – even though you may be quaking inside) is giving them a skill that will be of great use to them in later life.

So, first impressions count. I say again, what is the first thing your students see when they walk into your classroom? What is the first impression they get of you and your school each morning? What are you doing actively to develop positive relationships with the students in your class above the 'you're the student, I'm the teacher, we know our places, so let's get on with it' routine found in so many classrooms?

While we are on the subject, what is the last thing your students experience as they head out of the classroom at the end of the lesson or the end of the day? ('This is when I smile,' I hear you say.) If they go out feeling bored, scared, miserable, fed up or unmotivated they will bring those feelings back in with them next time they enter the classroom. After all, we memorise by association. Research conducted with divers in which they were taught certain nonsense words under water and then tested for recall showed that the divers who were also tested under water fared better than those who were tested on land. In other words, memories are linked to environment. Because of the sights, sounds and even smells in your classroom, the 'state' in which your students leave will be the 'state' in which they come back. Think about parents you see going back into a school environment for the first time for several years. See how some of them shrink down as they walk through the door, as they are hit by the smells and sounds that bring back so many memories.

> 'Any time you go back to somewhere where you've won you feel good about it.'

> Golf champion Laura Davies describing Phoenix, Arizona, but could it just as easily be your classroom?

Yet what do we do, certainly at GCSE or A-level? We take them out of the environment they have had for at least two years and to which so much of the learning is attached and, at least in my experience teaching French, put them in a big room that they normally associate with football, and which has weird lighting and that smells of socks, and then expect them to regurgitate the learning. The artificial process called academic learning we measure in an artificial way called an exam which we then conduct in an artificial way that distances the testing from the learning.

Why not take the students into the exam hall before the exams proper have started and do some review work with them so that they at least begin to associate the exam environment with the learning? Working on the premise that we have a fantastic visual memory, it has been suggested that you could even put posters up before the exams start, because then by looking at the blank piece of wall where the poster was they will more easily recall the learning from the poster. Remember the school at which staff hung a large white sheet from the climbing bars in the exam hall onto which students would 'project' their Mindmaps* in their mind's eye?

So the ethos that you create in the classroom works for you – or against you – from the moment they walk into the classroom and lasts well beyond the moment they walk back out, and a smile can be of such significance in that process, although there are other things.

Differences between sixth-form life and lower-school life

Go and wait by my office	Pop into the office any time for a chat
Take that make-up off	Your make-up looks nice today
That's not correct uniform	I like the skirt – a bit short though
I'll have those earrings	I just love those earrings
Detention at 4.30 pm	Barbecue at 4.30 pm

How we build walls pre-sixteen and bridges post-sixteen, according to students trying to market their new sixth form at a Catholic girls' school in London.

Listening to Professor Brighouse speak once, he identified a list of things we do in schools to build rapport with young people and let them know that we like them. My favourite item from his list was the fact that 'we steal from them'. When we nick a crisp from a child at lunchtime or cadge a sweet in the playground, we are doing more than saving ourselves the bother of buying our own snacks. We are addressing a fundamental part of our evolutionary psyche that says 'if I eat with you, I like you'.

Something else to share with young people as you build rapport with them is something far more precious than a bag of crisps – it is you. In other words, who you really are, not the teacher in the classroom. There is a fine line to tread here as I have seen teachers sharing information with young people in a way that simply made them cringe – 'Too much information, Miss!' – although I have also seen teachers talking about their own experiences in a way that really galvanised their class. One of the best assemblies I have ever attended involved a new head of year 10 talking about herself from the heart in a way that was honest but not too honest, frank but not too frank, open but just open enough. Similarly, in the work that I have seen tutors delivering on goal-setting in which the teacher is going through the motions without any actual emotional engagement, the lesson is usually a complete nightmare. Yet when he or she is talking about their own experiences there is a tangible creative tension in the classroom that brings the subject alive for the young people. And, of course, humour is hugely significant here too. Let them make you laugh, and vice versa.

> 'We are only given a little spark of madness. If you lose that you're nothing.'
>
> Robin Williams on why it's important for you to be you in your classroom.

In Chapter 7 we will see the need for instant feedback. To this, add the notion of personalised feedback, the idea that what they receive is especially for them, not just trite teacher clichés that you've churned out thousands of times before ('Maybe you should try harder too, Sir!'). For example, the use of students' names can be hugely significant (spell them properly and pronounce them well, even if it takes a little extra effort with names with which you are not familiar), and ensure that any celebrations and rewards you use are relevant to their likes and needs.

> 'I was in a group of seven in development engineering and we all got a raise the same day and we all got the same amount of money. And I thought I was a hell of a lot better than the other six. I didn't think it was a great deal.'

> Jack 'The Most Successful CEO Ever' Welch on meritocracy and the need for personalising praise.

Relationships between peers is a crucial element for having motivated learners too. What can be done to ensure that these are also being developed, again with a focus on the differences between students rather than trying to turn a class into one homogenous lump? A teacher who had started to introduce her students to multiple intelligence principles told me that it had really helped her class understand – and accommodate – the differences between each other. 'I don't like using music to learn,' one of her students said to her, 'but my friend does. So I'll do this musical exercise now because it will help him and next week we will be doing some maths work which he doesn't like but I do, so he will do it for me.'

I have so often found young people to be caring and considerate in this way but usually in a situation that combines a structure with a certain amount of freedom and control over what is going on. Peer mentoring is one example that seems to be effective here, as is mentoring between older children, such as sixth-formers, and the younger ones. Some of the smaller secondary schools have mixed-age tutor groups to good effect. Teachers at another primary school described how they had used multiple intelligences as a way of dividing the children into groups as opposed to doing it by ability. It gave the children the opportunity to see how everyone could contribute to a team and that a team has to be made of a range of different sorts of people with different skills, attitudes and areas of excellence.

> 'I truly believe that the way to be great is to associate with greatness.'

> Will Smith on why poor people should take rich people out to lunch.

An important message to reinforce to older students is how chameleon-like we are as human beings, that we become like who we spend time with. Or, as someone once put it to me in a fashion that is as memorable as it is controversial:

> If you want to fly with the eagles, don't scratch with the turkeys.

Does the student want to be successful, yes or no? Does he or she have a goal to work towards, yes or no? Are the people they are spending time with going to help them achieve that goal, yes or no? If no, what are they going to do about it?

'Life is too short to hang out with people who aren't resourceful.'

Amazon's Dave Bezos on how he plans his social life.

May I put the same question to you? Who are you spending time with? Who are you becoming like? Often when I am being briefed about delivering an INSET session in a school, reference is made to the 'staffroom cynics' – those teachers who seem to undermine any spark of energy or initiative with their 'been there, tried that, didn't work in 1957 so won't work now' mentality. They are the epitome of Milton Friedman's First Law of Bureaucracy – 'The only feasible way of doing anything is the way it is being done'. To be honest, you don't have to have been teaching for years to achieve TOM status ('Tired Old Men', as a colleague of mine refers to them, and note, as Thomas Edison said, 'Grouches are nearly always pinheads.'). I have met teachers fresh from college who are already so intransigent you could chain your bike to them. And, conversely, teachers who have seen many a summer holiday yet are still keen for new insights and ideas. My view is 'Avoid the cynics' and my main piece of advice to newly-qualified teachers is to keep out of the staffroom, hot-beds of cynicism and misery that they can be.

> 'All scientists know of colleagues whose minds are so well equipped with the means of refutation that no new idea has the temerity to seek admittance. Their contribution to science is accordingly small.'

Peter Medewar, writing in 1949, in *A Note on the Scientific Method*. Does it describe anyone you know?

> 'Cynicism is like a factory fire for organisations based on human capital.'

A quote from the people at St Luke's, the mould-breaking advertising agency, on the intellectual pyromaniacs in our midst.

Another way of building rapport with young people is to start 'where they are' and lead on from there, something referred to as 'CITV' or 'Connecting Into Their Values'. This may be, for example, the way I use the rich and famous as a way of harnessing students' attention before I go on to explain that there is far more to success than being rich and famous. A different example was when I used to say to a class, 'Red blood cells carry oxygen into the bloodstream and white blood cells fight off infection,' there could well be little to 'hook' these new concepts on to (remember pre-exposure from Chapter 2). They may have no previous knowledge and little in the way of visual images that come to mind to help ease the learning into their heads. So, what did they know that's red and white? Manchester United and angels! Imagine, then, the scene in which David Beckham (or whoever the current Manchester United superstar is) is dribbling down the bloodstream using an oxygen bubble for a football wearing a skirt, a headscarf, a thong and a Man. U shirt. Instantly, you show you have at least a basic knowledge of contemporary football (not to mention fashion), you have woken up their RAS, have linked into an aspect of life that is relevant and real to them and given them a visually memorable – and so, by definition, fantastically memorable – way of recalling what it is that red cells do.

For the white ones, imagine an angel in the bloodstream with a gun saying, 'Hey virus, make my day!' Not very academic you may say, and you may well be right. But if you are looking for ways of hooking in young people in a way that is fun and motivating, not to mention instantly memorable, then this does the trick.

The use of TV programmes, such as game shows, for revising is another example of tapping into their values (although I have yet to meet a careers teacher prepared to play Who Wants To Be a Milliner). Another example of this is something I have seen delivered by Jim Roberson, my friend from the Bronx, with a group of underachieving boys. In order to connect into their motivation we had set up an event which involved combining American football with learning and motivation work, alternating between the playing field and the classroom. Using a technique Jim calls 'crossover' he spoke to the boys using sporting terminology in relation to their exams. In other words, you are not 'revising' but 'in training' for your GCSEs, and he showed them that in the way that you wouldn't expect a team to peak at the beginning of the season, it should be the same with revision, turning up the heat consistently across the year until you reach the final/exams.

Another teacher I met who had ended up with an all-male bottom-set group for French used many sporting references throughout his teaching including Man of the Match awards at the end of each lesson and yellow and red cards for behaviour – 'Oh yes, my son is doing French at county level!'

I haven't met a child who isn't motivated, it's just that sometimes they are not motivated to do what we want them to do when we want them to do it. Yet by building the relationship to allow us to discover – and then go to – where their motivation already lurks we can take a short-cut in our lessons. After all, their brains are already wired up to two great driving forces in the human psyche – pain and pleasure. By understanding this you can tap into areas of motivation that are already there as they enter your classroom.

'I hate to lose more than I like to win.'

Tennis player Jimmy Connors on pain and pleasure and how much British tennis players must hurt.

A few years ago while keeping the wolf from the door with a spot of supply teaching I was asked to spend a period in the learning support classroom. On arriving they asked me to help a young lad in the corner with his reading. I sat down next to him (in those chairs which have been taken out of the staffroom when it was renovated ten years ago, with the strips of elastic under the cushion, except that by now there are only about two strips left so once you sit down you're wedged in with your backside almost touching the floor) and, without even looking up from his book, the student started to mumble his reading. I stopped him and shook his hand as I introduced myself to him, trying to break him out of what was obviously a 'hate reading, no good at it, don't want to be here' state. However, he immediately continued his mumbling, so I stopped him again and asked him, as I knew nothing about him, if he could tell me something he really enjoyed doing. In other words, I was looking for his 'pleasure button' (although I didn't say that to him). It turned out he was into aeroplanes in a big way so I asked him if he had ever sat in a cockpit. 'OK,' I continued, 'You're the pilot, I'm the co-pilot. That book is your joystick. Off you go, start reading,' and as he started reading I began to make aeroplane noises. He was beginning to smile now (the novelty of which was unnerving the special needs teacher) but then began to stumble over a certain word in his book. As he did this I began to make the noise of a plane in a critical dive! Like any good pilot working well under pressure he immediately sorted out the troublesome word and the aeroplane levelled off again, emergency over. He was in fits of giggles yet he was still reading and reading well. I had used the connections in his head – 'aeroplanes equals pleasure and reading equals pain' and started to 'rewire' them to link reading with pleasure (and because he was laughing I knew we hadn't simply linked aeroplanes to pain and turned off one of the few avenues of pleasure in his life). On another occasion when I was working in a primary school some of the girls were becoming unteachable (remember the reptilian brain) because of the rumbling of distant thunder. 'If it thunders I'll give you a merit,' seemed to do the trick.

What are the opportunities for you to work in a similar way with the young people you are involved with? Do you know what their likes and dislikes are? What are they already motivated to do? What already lights up the pleasure centres in their heads? It may not light your fire but, for now, that doesn't matter.

And, of course, the language you use will help you build rapport. I don't mean necessarily greeting them in a 'Yo, dudes!' sort of way but at very least communicating with them in a way that is somewhere near their own language. In a secondary school that had a high proportion of young people with learning difficulties I saw a sign in the boys' loos that read: 'Hygiene – It is important that toilets are flushed after use. Failure to do so not only causes inconvenience to others but could also spread diseases.' (Leading to verbal diarrhoea, I presume. Mind you, a sign that ran along the lines of 'These facilities are inspected regularly but if you feel that at any time they are clean and pleasant, please contact reception who will arrange for year 10 to come in and rectify the situation' is perhaps more appropriate.)

To a struggling year 7 boy such language must surely be yet another reinforcement of his failure to be part of what is going on. 'There is so much that I don't fully understand in the classroom and now I can't even take a leak without feeling stupid!'

'Rephrase please!'

A year 7 girl at a London school politely telling me that she didn't know what the hell I was going on about.

And while we are on the subject of language, there is nothing that undermines your relationships more than the use of teacher clichés, so if you ever find yourself about to utter such 'classics' as 'Would you do that at home?', 'I'm really disappointed in you',

'You're only cheating yourselves', 'We'll be in your time soon,' stop yourself immediately. There are stand-up comics making a living with these phrases and they are a great deal funnier than you are, so please desist!

In other words

- Invest your time in building relationships with your students.
- Smile and look like you want to be there.
- Be yourself in the classroom.
- Link into the motivation they already have.
- Help them understand the effects on their life of the people they spend time with.
- Watch your language – avoid teacher clichés.

Chapter 6

Reptiles in the classroom

'Fun?' the group of primary teachers suggested sheepishly, almost apologetically.

I often ask teachers what they suggest are their keys to having motivated learners in their classrooms. It was while doing this exercise in a London primary school once that I received the above response.

Oh, how we have strayed from the path of true learning when primary teachers have to ask permission to 'have fun' in the classroom, although when the inspectors call just refer to it as 'the use of positive emotions to access the limbic system'. Fun – and it's just one of a number of positive emotions we can employ – is not only useful, it is essential to learning, not as a bolt-on extra but as an integral part of learning. Why? Back to the brain …

There is a model for understanding the brain that has been around since the 1940s and, like many neurological models, works better these days as a metaphor rather than as an accurate description of brain functioning. Known as the Triune model, the theory, devised by Dr Paul Maclean in 1949 in the USA, divides the brain into three core parts – three brains in one, if you like – that mirror our evolution.

To take you through it, let's engage your 'kinaesthetic modality' as they say and ask you to do as follows if no one is looking. To create your own little model of the three-part brain, wrap one hand round a clenched fist made with the other hand

and hold it in front of you like a shadow puppet of a … hand wrapped round a clenched fist. The arm going up into the fists, think of as the spinal cord. The bottom wrist now is the part of your brain known as the reptilian brain, or brain stem, where you will find the five 'F's of basic human responses – fight, flight, flock, freeze and sex. Here, too, are other basic responses such as territorial and ritualistic behaviour. Think of the intelligence of a lizard – not feeling, not hypothesising, just getting by. What does a lizard need to be able to do to live a fulfilled and productive life? Stay alive and try to have sex – there's not much to it really. Think of the lizard as having the intelligence of a typical undergraduate.

The second part of the brain to evolve, so the theory went, was your bottom fist. Or to give it its full title, the limbic system. It is also known variously as the emotional brain or even the mammalian brain. Here we are working with emotions and here, too, are vital elements of our brain that help us lay down long-term memories. Long-term memory and emotion go together. You remember your first kiss. (But perhaps not your last, but then that's marriage for you!) Think of the intelligence of a dog. It does all that the lizard's brain can but, in addition, experiences emotions. Yet it cannot do the crossword. (A cat, on the other hand, will often be found curled up in the corner with a wordsearch.)

From your emotional brain, of which more later, we arrive at your top hand – the neocortex. This is the part that is proportionately so huge in humans, the bit with the squiggly lines, folds caused by the evolutionary scrunching up of an impressive surface area into a small space. Here are centres that deal with speech, processing new information, abstract thought and reasoning, the faculties that move us to the top of the evolutionary ladder. This is the part that moves beyond lizards and dogs and, yes, even most cats. (You can put your hands down now.)

It is in the interplay between the emotional brain and the neocortex that neuroscience and learning science are finally catching up with Plato when he wrote:

All learning has an emotional base.

Unless we emotionally believe something to be true, we do not fully believe it. Unless the emotional brain registers what the neocortex learns then it is not really believed. Otherwise, we would all be driving Skodas. Intellectually you know them to be fantastic cars these days. But emotionally … many just can't do it. Or, to give another example, have you ever known someone to be in a relationship that intellectually they/you know is no good for them/you but emotionally they/you just can't break free?

> 'Where thought conflicts with emotion, the latter is designed by the neural circuitry in our brains to win.'
>
> Rita Carter on why we wear those favourite clothes we should have thrown out years ago.

So what goes on in the subtle electrical and chemical interplay between these three areas of our brain when things start to hot up and we find ourselves unable and/or unwilling to cope with what life – or our French teacher – is throwing at us?

Essentially, we go 'reptilian'. The blood, the energy, the oxygen, all that fires the brain gets focused on our reptilian fight-or-flight brain. The brain 'downshifts'. It goes into 'survival' mode. And while it is there, don't expect it to give two hoots about the capital of Azerbaijan or the square of the hypotenuse. It is trying to work out how it can best avoid – or confront – the consequences of not having done this week's homework assignment, or being spotted by that big girl with a grudge in year 10 on the way home, or walking through the door to a drunk stepfather again.

> 'You can't run from a tiger with an erection!'
>
> The words of a PE teacher describing how he had been taught that our brains will choose survival over higher brain functions. Mind you, changing the first two words to 'You should … ' throws up a whole new survival scenario.

If I were to ask you to study a physics textbook while crossing a busy street at the same time, you would have to be heavily committed to the laws of motion to be able to resist moving into survival mode.

As with all neat theories about the brain it is far more complicated than this model would suggest, yet as a metaphor it is still very useful in a classroom scenario. One teacher I met had been told the following adage years ago by a former mentor of his, which not only reinforces this three-brains-in-one model, but also works at an empirical level:

> To teach you have to contain, entertain, explain. It doesn't work in any other order.

For the purposes of this chapter let's look at the first two.

Contain

The question here is quite simple – are we spending a great deal of time trying to teach children who have gone reptilian? The child in your classroom who is scared, hungry, insecure, vulnerable or exposed has got more important things with which to engage his or her neurological resources than consider the causes of coastal erosion or how to purchase cabbages in a far-off country.

> 'Having a praise-oriented manager rather than a punishment-oriented manager is very important for motivation – anybody who thinks you can motivate by fear is sadly mistaken.'
>
> Professor Cary Cooper on a key finding from his research into motivation, which has a message for Chief Inspectors of Schools everywhere.

To start at all, in true Maslov style, we need to address the basics, and have children warm and fed (does your school run a breakfast club, for example?) and free from fear. This also includes freedom from fear of failure (and see Chapter 4 for some ideas there), not to mention freedom from fear of another source of terror for some of your students – praise! Are there children in your classroom – possibly, especially, some of the boys – who are underachieving because they don't want to face the consequences of doing well? If we are looking at ways of helping young people to feel safe and unthreatened in our classrooms we have to consider the effects that praise, in all its various forms, will take. My son's 'punishment' for achieving 100 merits was the same as it had been for achieving fifty. He had to stand up in the middle of assembly and walk through a hundred or so of his peers to go to the front of the stage and have his hand shaken by the headteacher. He hated it! Yet it is supposed to be an incentive.

Look at it another way. Imagine that your school decided to operate a new incentive scheme to raise morale in the staffroom, something the head had seen in McDonald's. So, starting from Monday you are going to have a 'Teacher of the Week' award. When you win, your photo goes on display in the foyer and you receive a free bag of fries! How would you feel? It's hardly an incentive to excel, is it? And what you did achieve you would keep under your hat so as not to be singled out for the public humiliation that you would receive. (One primary teacher told me that in his previous school, every Friday afternoon, in whole-school assembly, the children were asked to raise their hands to vote for their favourite teacher that week! He didn't stay long.) If you would find such schemes too embarrassing for words, be aware that we may be putting children through exactly the same emotional treadmill without even being aware of it.

Given that we agreed in Chapter 3 that an element of choice is a key part in having happy and motivated learners in the classroom, I suggest you put the following question to any class you are working with.

When you do something really good, how would you like me to praise you?

Apart from giving them some choice in the matter, look out, as well, for some key presuppositions in that question, namely you *will* do something good – it's just a question of time – and I *will* see it.

Even the very word 'praise' may be worth re-evaluating. Remember Herzberg's KITA theory of motivation from the Introduction? On his list of keys to motivation at work he uses the term 'recognition', not praise, and there is a big difference. You don't want praise for everything that you do but you do want it to be recognised. When I was in my first year of teaching I helped a colleague plan and deliver a whole-school industry event, with everyone working on ways of transporting eggs for long distances (without simply throwing them, the more traditional means for that school). The event was a success and within a week I had received a little note – I still have it – from my colleague, thanking me for my support. This was worth far more to me than being singled out during a staff briefing for a round of applause, as could so easily have been the case.

One important tenet to remember in relation to this – especially, but not exclusively, when dealing with boys – is 'punish in private, praise in private'. Not wanting to look too keen is fine as a social survival strategy as long as the things are done that need to be done. We seem to spend a great deal of time trying to get young people to look 'enthusiastic' when the time could be better spent helping them take responsibility for the consequences of their actions. As Will Smith suggests, 'There's a psychological advantage to looking as if you're not trying too hard. But the truth is, while the other people are out playing around … I'm reading the script again.' That is the message worth trying to get through rather than making them have to look keen. I know one teacher who has a boy who never hands his homework in during the lesson when he is asked to but always brings it to her later that day when no one else is around.

> 'If you put the emphasis solely on winning people will first try to cheat. And secondly, they will try to win with the minimum of effort because that shows that they are even better.'

Motivation expert and *HR Magazine*'s '5th Most Influential Thinker in Human Resources in 2011' Professor Cary Cooper, who has obviously spotted those lads at the back of your classroom.

Other strategies include recognising their work with a little nudge or a smile that no one else sees. You may even keep them behind after the lesson to praise them in person and without an audience (something that also gives them the opportunity to rejoin their friends outside and boast how they were 'told off again'). One primary school sends out 'well done' postcards on a Friday afternoon so that they arrive at the children's homes on a Saturday morning.

Satisfying the reptilian brain also involves working with territorial behaviour. To address this think in terms of *their* place, *their* chair, *their* pen, *their* drawer, *their* classroom or form room, *their* work on the wall as appropriate – all of which gives them a sense of belonging.

Ritualistic behaviour is something else that is vital to work with in your classroom. In a world of chaos, rituals mean we know what is going to come next. Football chants, catch phrases, set-piece jokes, comic themes running through the day, funny songs, even simply a regular rhythm to the day – all of these contribute to our feelings of security and stability in the midst of a world where anything can happen at any minute. There are popular radio and TV shows that are essentially the same show at the same time with the same jokes delivered in the same way on a regular basis. Yet they are funny because of this.

Building rituals into your lessons means that you are working to satisfy a basic part of what makes us human – the way that you take the register, the way you offer praise when appropriate, common jokes and stories running from lesson to lesson, the way that you let them out at the end, that thing you always do every Thursday afternoon at 2.25 pm, whatever it may be (for example a joke, a story, a puzzle, a quiz, a Man of the Match award).

'VAK' your praise

Does your praise actually register in their brains anyway?

A headteacher told me once how not long after he had arrived at a new school there had been a Christmas concert organised by the music teacher. The event had been a great success and the head had put a note in his colleague's pigeonhole to thank him for such a brilliant night. Several weeks later he received a visit from the music teacher who put his head around the door of his office and asked hesitantly whether the head had enjoyed the concert. 'Of course, didn't you get the note?' the head replied, slightly confused. 'Yes, but I just wanted to make sure,' came the reply. The music teacher is likely to have had a strong auditory bias. When it came to the recognition for what he had achieved, hearing was believing, not seeing. How often may such a scenario be played out in classrooms – and staffrooms – across the land?

To 'VAK' your strategies for recognition too, seems to be the answer here (controversy over the term notwithstanding). Write the positive comments, give the smiley faces and the gold stars, smile as you praise them and look them in the eye when you do it. Show them you notice them. Yet, make sure you say what you think too. Tell them they are great. Have a fanfare as you read out the top marks for the test. Let them cheer as they do well. And help them to feel good: a pat on the back from you, from each other, from themselves (a good one in the primary classroom that I have seen in action – 'Pat yourselves on the back children, well done!'). Let's have a round of applause. Take a bow. Tell me how you feel to have done so well.

Once we have worked to satisfy the reptilian brain we can then move toward the limbic system.

Entertain

A useful word because it rhymes with contain and explain for the sake of the epithet but means a lot more than the teacher simply doing a good old song and dance routine (although that helps sometimes). What we are talking about here is the use of positive emotions in the classroom – *not as an optional extra* – but for the reasons I highlight above.

> 'It's hard to get good music out of an unhappy choirboy.'
>
> Edward Higginbottom, Director of the Choir of New College, Oxford, with a new motto for us all.

Fun, however, is just one of the positive emotions that we can use in the classroom (although it is a hugely important one for young people). Whenever researchers ask children what they are looking for in a good teacher, two things always seem to come up: (1) a sense of humour, and (b) consistency. Suspense, intrigue, curiosity, novelty, surprise, awe, passion, compassion, empathy, hitting goals, discovery, competition, overcoming obstacles, achievement, a sense of growth – all of these have a vital part to play in opening up the learning brain.

Why not to restrict play to playtime

The need for a playful environment in your classroom was reinforced in an article in the *Financial Times* in April 2000. In it, 'play' experts Patrick Bateson and Paul Martin argued the need for play in the workplace. 'The likely payback from play includes the acquisition and honing of physical and social skills, improved problem solving abilities, cementing personal relationships and fine-tuning the musculature and nervous system,' they stated. Taking us back to Chapter 3 and the need for choice, they pointed out that, 'activities are more likely to be perceived as play (and therefore attractive) rather than work (and therefore unattractive) if they are entered into voluntarily,' and added, as we learned in Chapter 1, 'motivation to play springs from within and the readiness to perform activities can be reduced by external rewards'. So, celebrate their efforts, don't simply bribe them.

We will take just a couple of those in more detail, but let's not start with curiosity as there is something very important to tell you about that, which you won't believe. I'll come back to curiosity in a minute …

No, only joking. Let's start with curiosity. Whether we like it or not we can't help but be curious. It's a survival instinct. Put a laboratory rat in a new environment (take it out of one cage and put it in a new one) and it will naturally explore. Where is the food, where are the exits, where might danger come from, where are the toilets? We work in a similar way and we can draw students out of themselves, whether they like it or not, by actively engaging their curiosity.

Imagine the scene; you are halfway through the TV news and just about to switch off for an early night when the newsreader says, 'Coming up later,' and all of a sudden you are sitting down again, waiting to see the amusing piece about the nun and the fireguard. It's the blatant use of curious human instinct to lure you in until the end of the programme. You can't escape it on the radio either. Commercial stations know that people switch off during the adverts. I do, and I used to write them. What they use to combat this, however, is a device that engages our natural curiosity, referred to in radio circles as 'throwing forward'. So, you'll hear things like, 'Coming up after the break, we'll find out what Edvard Greig used to keep in his pocket and rub for luck before a concert.' You're hooked. The use of hyperbole is useful here, too. Chris Evans is a master at this, saying things like, 'Coming up before 9.00, the funniest joke in the world,' or 'the best advert ever' or, one I remember distinctly was,

'Coming up before 8.30, the crudest thing anybody has said to anybody else ever!'

> 'The most successful scientists often are not the most talented, but the ones who are just impelled by curiosity.'
>
> Nobel prize-winning physicist Arthur Schawlow on the power of the inquisitive mind to change the world. Einstein, after all, started his journey when he was given a compass as a young man and became intrigued by how it could work, and look what happened to him.

Building such strategies into the classroom is a very simple and powerful motivator. At the beginning of the lesson outline your plans for the lesson – the big picture to satisfy the right brain – and then add that in twenty minutes you are going to give them a piece of information that will mean the difference between a D grade and a C grade at GCSE, for example, and ask them to remind you because you don't want to forget!

Novelty is another element of a motivating lesson. Because we have no memory of something novel the brain has to use higher areas in order to make sense of it. For us to remember things they need to be 'novel' and 'high contrast'. When things stand out they lure us in and they stick in our memories whether we like it or not. (This is why setting a meeting for 3.47 pm is more likely to have people turning up on time than saying 3.45 pm. In a lesson, give a deadline of seven minutes or three rather than five, which never usually means five.) The example I give to students is to ask them that if 100 people came in and introduced themselves one at a time, all called John, all wearing a grey suit, except for number 57 who was called Barry, and was wearing an orange suit and riding a donkey with a velvet hat, which one would they remember?

So, how many orange Barrys on his donkey are there in your schemes of work? How many things that they were least expecting? Those events, from time to time, that make your lessons memorable? Do your students know the format of the lessons you are about to deliver – not, perhaps, the content, but very much the process that they will go through? If so, what can you do, as the Americans say, to 'throw them a curve ball'? Or, as we English say, 'bowl them a googlie' (a phrase I understand even less than the American one, come to think of it).

The galvanising effect on our motivation and memory of outstanding events is a phenomenon known as the Von Restorff effect. When faced with something that we least expect, the brain seems to take a snapshot of what was happening just before it and immediately after it. Examples of the Von Restorff effect can be seen with the death of JFK or Princess Diana or 9/11. The emotional reaction caused by the nature of an event is what is involved in making an event memorable. Short-term memory (making it to the telephone from the directory with the number still in your head, the bit of background music you listened to five minutes ago on the radio, the fact that it's your turn to take out the wheelie bin) is predominantly a fleeting chemical electrical flash in our brains, transitory certainly to our conscious brain. A long-term memory, however, is an actual physical change in the very structure of the brain. How does the brain know what to make into a long-term memory and what to let pass as a brief flash? The answer would appear to be the chemical triggers released by our emotions. Without emotions there are no – or at least far fewer – triggers to send the message to the brain: this stuff is important, remember it.

So, whichever way you look at it, the need for positive emotions has to be an integral part of your lessons and planned for as part of your responsibility in helping manage and maintain the optimum state for learning (along with breathing, energy, movement and the other things we are discussing in this book). Then, and only then, can we complete our journey from 'contain' to 'entertain' to 'explain'. Here, arriving at the neocortex, we can now work with the intellectual processing of new ideas, the recognition and processing of new stimuli, the manipulation of abstract concepts and the processing of language – safe ground in the traditional classroom.

In other words

- Role model having fun and taking risks.
- Use the 'contain, entertain, explain' model.
- Engage a variety of positive emotions.
- 'VAK' your praise.
- Actively engage their curiosity.
- Throw in things from time to time they would be least expecting.

Chapter 7

Motivation is a four-letter word

Hope fires a neuron.

It was Professor John MacBeath, professor Emeritus at Cambridge University (and a great champion of the sorts of thinking on which we have been focusing here) whom I first heard use this phrase. I don't think it was an original line to him but he was certainly making it clear to the audience present that the process of feeling hopeful changes things in our brains. When we are in a state of hopefulness our brains literally light up with electrical energy coursing around the upper – intellectual – regions. However, when we find ourselves in a state of hopelessness the brain will dim with the energy downshifting, as we mentioned before, to the lower, more basic, do-the-bare-minimum-to-survive elements.

> 'Sometimes my life has been a dark tunnel, but I'm here, I've survived. I believe that there is hope, and that you can be happy if you work at it.'
>
> Mackenzie Thorpe on what can be achieved with hope – take another look at the front cover of this book. Is that your school pictured there?

Imagine your students' heads are transparent and that when you are working with them you can see the electrical activity flashing around each individual cranium. Watch as your positive comment – 'You'll go far' – or rewarding look or little nudge simply lights up their brain.

Alternatively, watch as you chase away all hope with your disparaging comments – 'Maths isn't really your thing is it?'; 'I don't think you'll make it as a poet'; 'Call that a sheep?'

Are you a hope giver or a hope taker? Do your students walk away from your classroom with higher levels of hope and optimism than when they walk in?

Hope works on our brains and bodies in a number of ways. In his book *Emotional Intelligence* Daniel Goleman describes research conducted into the benefits of having high levels of hope and optimism. It has been shown in students who outperformed peers at university with higher IQ scores but lower hope scores, in insurance salespeople who did not make it through the psychometric testing at interview stage yet when employed anyway for the purposes of the experiment still outperformed 'better suited' colleagues with lower hope scores, and in victims of heart disease and cancer who outlived by years other patients with the same prognosis but lower levels of hope. Hope changes things in our brains and in our bodies.

Bear in mind as well that research shows that when our right brains are more dominant we can end up feeling more depressed, negative or stressed. Yet with the left brain in control we tend to be more optimistic about the future, reinforcing the need to teach optimism, including goal-setting, conflict resolution, purpose, vitality, vision and hope.

The question, then, is what are you doing to manage and maintain high levels of hope in your classroom *despite the immediate evidence*? Even though everything leading up to today implies the student 'isn't too bright', what can you do differently today so that you get a different result tomorrow? After all, remember, if you do the same thing today that you did yesterday, you'll end up with the same result tomorrow. Or, in management speak, if you always do what you've always done, you'll always get what you've always got.

When I was teaching French we were encouraged to have the C/D borderline GCSE students back in school, after school, in their own time to work with them to raise their potential grades. However, all that we did was do more of the same. The same strategies that were used in school were used again after school. These students became very successful C/D borderline French students. We practised repeatedly how *just* to fail French. And they all did. Just. They were some of the best D grades in the country; I was very proud.

What could we have done differently? This throws up the sorts of strategies and ideas we have been focusing on throughout this book. When Professor MacBeath was asked to look into how effective after-school clubs were at raising achievement, one of the things that came through was the need to look outside the traditional methods of teaching in order to make a difference. His report suggested that schools needed to consider aspects including self-esteem and self-confidence and that strategies relating to accelerated learning should be considered too. In other words, more of the same but harder was not going to make a difference.

If a student does an essay and receives a D grade and is told to do it again and then proceeds to do it in exactly the same way, what is going to happen? And then the student walks away, head down, 'knowing' that he or she is 'just a D grade student'. What, however, could they do differently? Now it's time to put creative-thinking hats on. Ask the teacher for more specific guidance. Ask someone who has a better grade how they did it. Find someone older who may have done it last year to help. At the very least, dig out some different resources and plan the essay in a different way.

It doesn't sound like rocket science, yet I see so many people in schools – young and not so young – fighting the same battles over and over again and looking for different results. There is a phrase from creative-thinking circles that says, 'Nothing is more dangerous than an idea when it is the only idea you've got.' Remember the large, grey elephant from Chapter 2? The more we can encourage young people to develop a creative attitude of divergent thinking, the more we can help them avoid the 'tried it, didn't work, can't do it' attitude. And, apart from the creative-thinking strategies, we need to encourage them to have the sorts of levels of hope that will keep them optimistic in the face of apparent failure.

'Try to have a thought of your own, thinking is so important.'

Is Blackadder's message to the hapless Baldrick one you agree with? Or does your school have, like Bart Simpson's, an 'Independent Thought' alarm to nip such practices in the bud?

Creativity and self-esteem

One of the first classes to which I taught creativity was a group of prisoners from a maximum security prison in Leicestershire, and it was here that I learned that there are more benefits to creative thinking than simply becoming more creative. One of the delegates was, shall we say, not a regular on the school photo yet he was very motivated in the creativity classroom. After the course he came up to me to explain why: 'For the first time ever my ideas counted! Even though he [the delegate next to him who had been part-way through a university degree before his crime] had been to university my ideas were just as important.'

Apart from the range of creative-thinking strategies he had learned, he was walking out of the classroom with his head held high for the first time ever, thanks to a process that says there are no rights or wrongs.

I was good at the 'guess what is in the teacher's head' type question-and-answer game at school. I am sure most teachers were. Do we know what it feels like to be scared of opening our mouths for fear of being told we are wrong or stupid or both? Opportunities for creative thinking help everyone to feel good about answering. I know there are times when students need to know specific answers but, in arriving at those answers, are there opportunities for creative brainstorming (these days referred to in thinking skills circles as 'generative thinking'), freewheeling ideation that gives everybody a chance to succeed?

The seven rules of effective brainstorming

The seven rules of effective brainstorming according to Ideo, recognised as the world's most creative design consultancy (from Apple's first mouse to a mechanical whale for *Free Willie*):

1   Defer judgement.
2   Build on the ideas of others.
3   Stay focused on the topic.
4   One person at a time.
5   Go for quantity (150 ideas in a 30 to 45-minute session).
6   Encourage wild ideas.
7   Be visual.

Does this describe a typical management team meeting in your school? Or is every new idea strangled at birth? Or perhaps you prefer blamestorming … ?

Generating answers without fear of failure helps with motivation, as does the quality of feedback and response from the teacher, an area in which we can learn a great deal from video games. I often hear comments about the lack of 'stickability' in boys, in particular, that they fail and then give up. Yet watch a boy – as I have done with my son – playing a computer game and you see a different side to his character. Despite being vaporised repeatedly by, say, the evil Krug, he seems to pick himself up and keep on trying until he comes out on top, completes the level and then moves on to bigger and bloodier challenges.

Apart from the way that such computer games tie into basic urges in the psyche of young males, for better or for worse, one of the other aspects is the quality and timing of the feedback they provide. Instantly boys know *if* what they have done is right or wrong, instantly they know *what* it is they have done right or wrong and they can instantly pick themselves up and get back on with the game again. In the classroom, feedback tends to come in a different way and, most demotivating of all, it tends to be far from immediate. 'Do your homework on Tuesday night, hand it in on Wednesday afternoon, find out how you did the following Monday,' is hardly instant feedback. A computer game that lets you know a week later whether you had been blasted by the evil Krug would not be a bestseller.

What are the opportunities for instant feedback in your lessons, along with the 'delayed gratification' opportunities that we discussed in Chapter 3? One teacher told me how in his school they had decided that they were fed-up doing so much marking in their own time until late into the night and so had resolved not to do it any more. With creative-thinking hats on they now plan lessons with a great deal more marking on the spot, self- and peer-marking, with opportunities for the teacher to go around the class during lessons looking at books from time to time.

Instant feedback, peer work, a sense of control and responsibility for the students, and an early night for the staff – what more can you want? Notice here, by the way, how the frustration with an unsatisfactory situation, when channeled effectively, will produce creative ideas. In other words, use your frustrations as a lever to create a better reality. As Freud said:

> We may lay it down that a happy person never phantasies, only an unsatisfied one. The motive force of phantasies are unsatisfied wishes and every single phantasy is the fulfillment of a wish, a correction of an unsatisfying reality.

Nuph said!

> 'You need lots of unfulfilled ambitions to keep you motivated.'
>
> Former CEO of United Biscuits Leslie Van de Walle on frustration and the motivational benefits derived, appropriately, from biting off more than you can chew.

> 'I hope that I may always desire more than I can accomplish.'
>
> Michelangelo, who achieved a great deal, so heaven knows what he actually desired!

There are a number of other ways in which I try to work towards this crucial sense of hope in young people. As with so many things, let's go back to our understanding of the brain, in particular our understanding of what we mean by potential.

Every school, I have noticed, somewhere in its blurb says something along the lines of, 'We aim to bring out the *full potential* of all our children.'

Hogwash!

Are you working to *your* full potential? One of the first questions British business guru and 'troubleshooter' Sir John Harvey Jones used to ask employers when he met them was, 'What proportion of your capability is being used?' No one, he claimed, ever offered him more than around 20 per cent. And that was high, he used to point out! And then we say to children, 'You're not working to your full potential.' (And they say, 'Well, neither are you Miss,' and you say, 'Shh, be quiet, let that be our little secret.')

> 'The mind is not large enough to contain itself.'
>
> St Augustine on how none of it is all in our heads.

What exactly do we mean by potential? Remember how the brain learns by making new connections and how the more connections we make, the more connections we *can* make (from Chapter 2)? Working on this premise, the brain experts sat down and tried to figure out what the potential for making connections is in the average healthy human brain. In other words, what is our potential for learning, as a number? I have come across a variety of estimates of this figure, stretching, literally, from a 'one' followed by a line of zeros that goes on for 10.5 million kilometres to a number that is bigger than the number of atoms in the visible universe. Baroness Susan Greenfield's version is that if the brain cells were the trees in the Amazon rainforest and the connections were the leaves, counting the number of leaves on all the trees would take thirty-one million years. In other words, it would take thirty-one million years to count the potential for learning of your apparently least-able child. Bear that in mind next time you are in the staffroom and hear your colleagues describe a child as stupid.

As a percentage there are various estimates of how much of this huge potential we use and, in many ways, it is an impossible question to answer, although 'guesstimates' vary from as high as twelve per cent, in an advert I saw recently in an American business magazine, to less than one per cent, suggested by Tony Buzan. The most important thing to remember here, however, is not the maths but the idea that whatever you have achieved in the past you can achieve more. Because, whatever you achieved in the past was just, let's say, two per cent of what you are really capable of.

> You have ninety-eight per cent of the world's most powerful piece of equipment sitting between your ears just waiting, wasted.

Neuroscience aside, that alone is the sort of sentence that can change your life. Even if the neuroscience changes and the experts conclude that we do use a lot more of our potential for learning than was first thought, it doesn't matter. It doesn't matter because that sentence is a statement of a belief and a belief doesn't have to be true or false to be effective. As long as we believe it, it is true and it is with such beliefs that we mould and change our lives.

> 'If I didn't die yesterday and I'm alive today then tomorrow will be great.'

> The belief system of a blind, poor Ghanaian farmer talking on Radio 4 – pin it up in the staffroom next time you have an inspection.

There are so many ways in which our beliefs decide our reality. What do you believe a good lesson looks like? Some – many – teachers will describe a good lesson as one in which the students are sitting down, often in rows, heads over their books, with a quiet murmur of noise going on. Not, perhaps, a good drama lesson. An alternative belief to that is a line from Eric Jensen which powerfully shapes the work that I do with young people:

> Learning is messy.

Take that on board as a belief and, without having to throw out academic rigour and effective classroom management, you will find a great deal more flexibility for teaching and a greater awareness of the many ways in which learning can take place in a classroom.

So many times in school I come across teachers who tell me that they would really like to try to do things differently in their classrooms and have the children up and moving around and playing music, and the like, but they are really worried that the headteacher is going to walk down the corridor, look in the window and tell them off. However, in the same schools I speak to the head who describes how he walks down the corridors, looks in the windows and is appalled by how boring the teaching is, and how he wishes the teachers would have the students up and dancing about and using music, etc., etc.

A good starting point for introducing change into your school is to ask each member of staff to complete the following sentence, 'A good lesson is … ' and see what happens. It will give you a real insight into the beliefs that your colleagues have about what teaching and learning *should* look like.

What are the beliefs that you have about the children in your school? So many schools will excuse the underachievement of their students with the tried and tested 'What do you expect from the kids from round here?' excuse. But for every 'kids from round here' school I come across, I will encounter another one, just down the road, with the same kids from the same 'round here' doing twice as well.

A school's beliefs are usually summed up in a 'vision statement', a process best encapsulated at a school in Peterborough in which underneath such a statement pinned up in the foyer someone had written 'Top Secret'! While they can be powerful documents when done well they often are neither. How long is it for a start? Bill Gates says that you need a vision you can 'keep in one brain'. And if I stopped a student/teacher/parent/governor in the street and asked them to recite your school's vision, could they? A game I play in my INSET events, from time to time, is to ask the teachers to make up some examples of the 'World's Worst School Vision Statement'. Choose one of these to go above your doors:

- This week's blitz is …
- Grades 'r' Us.
- Obedience before imagination.
- Evil be to year 8.
- Excellence through selection (this works best in Latin).
- Doing our best – considering.
- Community College – Keep Out.

What are the beliefs you have about yourself and your school? Do you believe you are working in a school that is – *or has the potential to be* – 'as good as the best in the world', to borrow a phrase from Jack Welch? If you don't, then you always have an excuse to underachieve. And what about you? Do you believe that you are – or could be – one of the best teachers in the world? To quote Sir John Harvey Jones, 'The only thing to aim for is being the best in your field in the bloody world.'

On the subject of beliefs, what are the beliefs of the children leaving your presence at the end of the day, or leaving your school at the end of their time there? No matter what it says on paper, if they believe that they are capable of a great deal and the world's their oyster, then that is the reality they will end up with. If, again, no matter what it says on paper, they believe that they are not really that clever and that they can't do this and can't do that and that this is 'as good as it gets,' then that is the reality they will end up with. After all, I meet many adults who will say that they are 'not that clever' and, when challenged, will justify the belief with the fact that they didn't do very well at school *thirty years ago*. It's never as good as it gets unless we accept that this is as good as it gets.

It's important for me to get this message across as soon as possible in my work because, before I can go on to describe how to learn, students must at least feel that they can learn – no matter what has happened before.

Beliefs and the Parking God

Do you believe in the Parking God? Some do, although you might not know it as such. Believing in the Parking God means that, wherever you are going in the car, if you confidently expect there to be a parking space exactly where you want it, when you want it, you will find that space. One teacher I met knew it as the Parking Fairy. Another teacher told me how her brother-in-law used it for 'parking' jet fighters in the RAF, which meant that whenever she and her husband went to the shops they would work on the premise that 'if Geoff can find a space for a Tornado, then we can find a space for our Ford Escort'. Yet another teacher recently explained that she had once been told that if you drive looking for a parking space with the tip of your tongue pushing against the back of your top teeth, then you will always find a space. And she did.

If our beliefs can find us parking spaces, if pushing our tongue against our teeth can change our life, what else can our beliefs help us to achieve?

Here is a two-part question in relation to hope for you to try with your colleagues:

> What can you do, and what could you do, in relation to building hope and optimism with your students?

Be aware that there will be things you are doing already that are hitting the right 'hope buttons'. I am sure that some of your students will be like the thousands I have seen whose levels of hope and optimism are through the roof – like the little girl who was asked by the inspector whether she could swim, to which she replied, 'Yes, but not yet.'

What else could you do is, though, another important question. There are so many students passing through the 'hope' net. I meet them so often, usually in the bottom-set groups and when asked to do a task they simply reply, 'I can't do that, I'm thick. I'm in the bottom set, didn't they tell you?' They believe it and, again, our beliefs decide our reality.

In my French classroom at one point I put four blank sheets of paper above the board and was met with the desired curiosity by my classes. A few weeks later I wrote the word 'You' on the first one, a few weeks after that I wrote the word 'can', a few weeks after that the word 'do'. And a few weeks later, for those who hadn't yet twigged, the word 'anything' (with a little footnote, 'but not in my classroom!'). I wanted my students to understand that *even though* they might struggle with French, they could still be somebody significant in the world. Yet the message they were leaving with, if I was not careful, was: 'You're no good at French so you're no good.' Which, of course, was quite simply not true.

I felt that it was important to get across to them the message that just because they couldn't conjugate a verb in a foreign language that they didn't want to learn in the first place it didn't mean they were less of a human being with less potential for success. And for some of these students I felt sure that the message they were receiving elsewhere was similar – 'You're no good at maths so you're no good', 'You're no good at English so you're no good', 'You're no good at PE so you're no good', 'In fact you're no good all round. Now, off you go, have a good life.' And this was in a school where the motto was 'Quality and Excellence for All'.

What do you do – or could you do – in word or deed, to raise levels of hope and optimism with your students? I am aware, by the way, that parents have a part to play in this process, too, with some being great hope stealers, even from children at an early age. A primary school in Watford told me once that one of their 5-year-olds was referred to at home as the 'stupid cow'. Isn't that appalling? Less obscene but equally insidious was the parent who told me that her son was like a lighthouse in the desert. When I asked her what she meant she said, 'He's bright but useless!'

> 'If you become a soldier, you'll be a general, if you become a monk, you'll end up as Pope.'
>
> Mrs Picasso Senior to the young Pablo, with a lesson for us all on having high expectations for our children.

That said, I also know that teachers are in the job of changing lives. The mission of my company, Independent Thinking, is,

'To enrich the lives of young people by changing the way they think and so to change the world.' Very grand, you may think, but that could equally be the mission of every school and every teacher in every school throughout the land. We can all think of one teacher in our lives who believed in us when no one else did or saw in us something that no one else saw. That was all it took to make us – and consequently the world – different. After all, it was a PE teacher who asked a 13-year-old lad one day in school whether he would like to try a spot of rowing – and we all know what happened to young Redgrave from there.

> 'A teacher affects eternity, he can never tell where his influence stops.'
>
> Henry B. Adams on how the power you have – for better or for worse – lasts well after the bell has gone. Ensure you use your power for good. According to William Sanders at the University of Tennessee in 1992, 'a single ineffective teacher can thwart a child's progress for at least 4 years'.

The 'Anything Possible World' we visited in Chapter 1 is another useful strategy here for raising hope levels too, the belief that anything is possible and that they can make it happen.

And one final angle I take is the stories about people in all walks of life who have achieved amazing things despite an inauspicious start at school. Einstein was unexceptional at school and it is said that he was a late speaker and a late reader. In fact, when asked why he didn't speak until quite late in infancy he is said to have replied, 'Because I didn't have anything to say.' Winston Churchill was quoted as saying 'Exams are a torture to me,' and was, I believe, chained to his desk at school.

It is the same from the world famous to the less well known but still remarkable. My insurance salesman friend is one. He left school with a CSE in technical drawing and was told by his careers teacher that, as he was good with his hands, he should go and be a bricklayer. (Like the boy who was advised that as he had O-levels in RE and woodwork, he should go and be an undertaker!) However, rather than be any old bricklayer, my friend decided he wanted to be the best bricklayer around and that he would brick-lay for England. I didn't know there was an all-England bricklaying team but there is. He won a cup and put it on the mantelpiece he had built. Then he thought to himself, 'If I can do this what else can I do?' to which the answer was, 'Own a sports car.' Not long after that he went into insurance, not because he desperately wanted to be an insurance salesman, but because he knew it would move him nearer to his goal. (Remember Question 3 from Chapter 4.) He was recently a member of the MDRT – the Million Dollar Round Table – a prestigious hall of fame for successful insurance professionals. Last time I met him he said that, as the government had introduced a raft of new qualifications for people in the financial world, he had a number of tricky new exams to take. He passed first time, but many of his graduate colleagues failed and had to re-sit. And he recently told me that he was dyslexic! If a dyslexic brickie with a CSE in technical drawing can fly this high, then what can the rest of us achieve?

> 'You could be the world's best garbage man, the world's best model; it don't matter what you do if you're the best.'
>
> Advice on being the best from the Greatest – Muhammad Ali.

Another similar example is the story of Richard Branson, a man who claims to be useless with numbers (I read recently of an incident during a finance meeting in which his colleagues had to stop proceedings to explain to him that of all the fish in the Atlantic, the ones in the net were the ones he got to keep. Think net and gross!); a dyslexic ('My early problems with dyslexia made me more intuitive', he says in his autobiography, citing how his dyslexia actually helped with his success in later life, although the idea that he didn't know how dyslexic he was until he went to a toga party dressed as a goat is entirely fictitious. For a veritable Who's Who of stars with dyslexia check out www.famousdyslexicpeople.com and show the glittering list to any struggling young person); and, by his own admission on Radio 1, explaining his link up with Bill Gates for the National Lottery bid, 'computer illiterate'. I'm not saying that literacy, numeracy and ICT are not useful, but perhaps there are some more fundamental issues to get right first.

Success and money

Sometimes, because of the people that I focus on when talking about success, I am criticised by certain teachers for encouraging young people to equate success solely with money. This is very much not the case, although I do use certain names to grab their attention (remember the RAS?) rather than sticking to the moral high ground and wondering why I'm all alone. 'Go to where they are and then lead them onwards from there' seems to me to be a useful way of working with young people. Rich and famous names grab their attention. Once you have that, the real teaching can begin.

One of the quotes that I share with them is a Branson one from America's *Fortune* magazine, yet it is the antithesis of the financial avarice the publication's title suggests. Asked about his attitude on success and taking risks he says at one point, 'It's not a question of making two or three billion dollars, it's a question of not wasting one's life.' And, for a similar perspective from a very different place, consider the words of Helen Keller when she said, 'Life is either a daring adventure or it is nothing.' Perhaps the remarkable learning story of Helen Keller is a good place to leave you. Although, perhaps I can throw one more idea into the pot for you to think about before I go – consider the humble Jammie Dodger.

A number of schools that I go into these days are beginning to look at some of the strategies covered in this book and teachers will say things like, 'Oh yes, we do multiple intelligences,' or 'We do VAK,' which is excellent news and a far cry from even just a few years ago. (Staff in some schools say, 'We know this,' as if that is all that is needed, forgetting that, 'We do this,' is actually the key to making it work. A teacher I met from a secondary school in the West Midlands told me how they had 'looked' at multiple intelligences for two years and 'surveyed' the children's learning styles and 'observed' what was going on. Paralysis by analysis I think it's called.) Think of the strategies as the biscuit around the jam, important, useful, effective. Yet a bunch of strategies does not a Jammie Dodger make. There is also the matter of the jammy heart to be addressed. Here are the issues relating to hope and aspirations, expectations and beliefs, unconditional acceptance of and, yes, even love of, the young people in your class. I can be a science teacher who has taken on board the principles of multiple intelligences and planned a lesson accordingly but unless I have a *fundamental belief in the limitless potential* of the students in front of me, I will still be limiting myself, not to mention my students.

We have many headteachers – we also need to ensure we have heart–teachers too.

> 'The history of the world has been the history of the victory of the heartless over the mindless.'
>
> Sir Humphrey Appleby on why we should say, 'No, Prime Minister,' from time to time.

Hopefully this book has helped you look at the true essence of motivation in your classroom – the jammy heart as well as the strategic biscuit, so to speak. I know that the ideas in *Essential Motivation* can and do make a difference to help young people achieve something closer to their potential in schools, outside of schools and, even more importantly, beyond school.

And, if you are looking for a message to reinforce this in a way that may help you with your levels of hope in the way that is does for me, I hand the last word over to Nelson Mandela. In his book *The Long Walk to Freedom* he says this:

> Education is the great engine of personal development. It is through education that the daughter of a peasant can become a doctor, that the son of a mineworker can become the head of the mine, that a child of farm workers can become the president of a great nation. It is what we make out of what we have, not what we are given, that separates one person from another.

In other words

- Ensure you are doing all you can to develop and maintain high levels of hope.
- Bear in mind what you can do to help your community with its hope levels too.
- Set up opportunities, such as effective brainstorming sessions, for everyone to succeed in your classroom.
- Make sure your school has a 'vision' and ensure that everyone knows what it is.
- Teach to 'hearts and minds' as well as the brains of all your students.
- Have a biscuit.

Bibliography

Abbott, J. and Ryan, T. (2000) *The Unfinished Revolution*, Stafford: Network Educational Press.

Bach, R. (1973) *Jonathan Livingston Seagull*, London: Pan Books.

Branson, R. (1998) *Losing My Virginity*, London: Virgin Publishing.

Buzan, T. (1989) *Use Your Head*, London: BBC Books.

Carter, R. (1998) *Mapping the Mind*, London: Weidenfeld & Nicolson.

Claxton, G. (1997) *Hare Brain Tortoise Mind*, London: Fourth Estate.

Covey, S.R. (1992) *The Seven Habits of Highly Effective People*, London: Simon & Schuster.

Csikszentmihalyi, M. (1992) *Flow*, London: Rider.

Dougan, A. (1998) *Robin Williams*, London: Orion Media.

Dryden, G. and Vos, J. (1994) *The Learning Revolution*, Torrance, CA: Jalmar Press.

Dyson, J. (1998) *Against the Odds*, London: Orion Business.

Edwards, B. (1979) *Drawing on the Right Side of the Brain*, East Rutherford, NJ: Putnam Publishing Group.

Fischer, L. (1997) *The Life of Mahatma Gandhi*, London: HarperCollins Publishers.

Gardner, H. (1993) *Multiple Intelligences – The Theory in Practice*, New York: Basic Books.

Gardner, H. with Laskin, E. (1997) *Leading Minds*, London: HarperCollins Publishers.

Gazzaniga, M. (1994) *Nature's Mind: Biological Roots of Thinking, Emotions, Sexuality, Language and Intelligence*, New York: Basic Books.

Gates, B. (1995) *The Road Ahead*, New York: Viking Penguin.

George, D. (1997) *Gifted Education, Identification and Provision*, London: David Fulton Publishers.

George, D. (1997) *The Challenge of the Able Child*, 2nd edn, London: David Fulton Publishers.

Gibran, K. (1992) *The Prophet*, London: Penguin Group.

Goleman, D. (1996) *Emotional Intelligence*, London: Bloomsbury Publishing.

Greenfield, S. (1997) *The Human Brain*, London: Weidenfeld & Nicolson.

Greenfield, S. (2000) *Brain Story*, London: BBC Worldwide.

Grinder, M. (1991) *Righting the Educational Conveyor Belt*, Portland, OR: Metamorphous Press.

Gruneberg, M.M. (1987) *Linkword Language System: French*, London: Transworld Publishers.

Handy, C. (1995) *The Age of Unreason*, London: Arrow Books.

Handy, C. (1996) *Beyond Certainty*, London: Arrow Books.

Hannaford, C. (1995) *Smart Moves*, Arlington, VA: Great Ocean Publishers.

Hayman, S. (1999) *You Just Don't Listen: A Parent's Guide to Improving Communication with Young People*, London: Random House.

Herzberg, F. (1968) 'One more time – how do you motivate employees?', *Harvard Business Review*, No. 68108; republished in a compendium (1991) *Business Classics: Fifteen Key Concepts for Managerial Success*, Boston, MA: Harvard Business School Publishing.

Jackson, T. (1995) *Virgin King*, London: HarperCollins Publishers.

Jensen, E. (1995) *The Learning Brain*, Del Mar, CA: Turning Point Publishing.

Jensen, E. (1995) *Super Teaching*, Del Mar, CA: Turning Point Publishing.

Jensen, E. (1996) *Brain-Based Learning*, Del Mar, CA: Turning Point Publishing.

Jensen, E. (1996) *Completing the Puzzle: The Brain-Based Approach*, Del Mar, CA: Turning Point Publishing.

Jones, D. (2000) *Almost Like a Whale*, London: Anchor (Transworld Publishers).

Lewis, C. (1994) *The Unemployables*, Chalford, UK: Management Books 2000.

MacBeath, J. (1998) *Extending Opportunity: A National Framework for Study Support*, London: DfEE.

McCormack, M.H. (1986) *What They Don't Teach You At Harvard Business School*, London: Fontana Paperbacks/William Collins.

McGuiness, C. (1999) *From Thinking Skills to Thinking Classrooms*, Norwich: The Stationery Office.

Maltz, M. (1960) *Psycho-Cybernetics – A New Way to Get More Living Out of Your Life*, New York: Pocket Book Editions.

Martin, P. (1998) *The Sickening Mind*, London: HarperCollins Publishers.

Mosley, L. (2000) *Lindbergh: A Biography*, New York: Dover Publications.

Noble, A. (ed.) (2000) *The Little Book of Sayings of Oscar Wilde*, Bath: Parragon.

Nordström, K. and Ridderstråle, J. (2000) Funky Business, London: Pearson Education.

Ostrander, S. and Schroeder, L., with Ostrander, N. (1994) *Super-Learning 2000*, New York: Dell Publishing.

Peters, T. (1994) *The Tom Peters Seminar*, London: Macmillan.

Peters, T. (1995) *The Pursuit of WOW!*, London: Macmillan.

Pinker, S. (1998) *How The Mind Works*, London: Allen Lane/The Penguin Press.

Pritchett, P. (1995) *The Employee Handbook of New Work Habits for a Rapidly Changing World*, Washington: Pritchett and Associates.

Rand, A. (1994) *The Fountainhead*, London: HarperCollins Publishers.

Richardson, K. (1999) *The Making of Intelligence*, London: BCA (by arrangement with Weidenfeld & Nicolson).

Robbins, A. (1988) Unlimited Power, London: Simon & Schuster.

Robertson, I. (1999) *Mind Sculpture*, London: Transworld Publishers.

Rose, C. (1985) *Accelerated Learning*, Aylesbury: Accelerated Learning Systems.

Rose, S. (1992) *The Making of Memory*, London: Transworld Publishers.

Scruton, R. (2000) *The Financial Times*, the business FT weekend magazine, 28 October, p. 37.

Sharron, H. and Coulter, M. (1994) *Changing Children's Minds*, Birmingham: Imaginative Minds.

Index